I0198178

THE RIVALS

AND

THE SCHOOL FOR SCANDAL

Macmillan's Pocket American and English Classics

A Series of English Texts, edited for use in Elementary and Secondary Schools, with Critical Introductions, Notes, etc.

16mo   Cloth   25 cents each

Addison's Sir Roger de Coverley.
Andersen's Fairy Tales.
Arabian Nights' Entertainments.
Arnold's Sohrab and Rustum.
Austen's Pride and Prejudice.
Bacon's Essays.
Bible (Memorable Passages from).
Blackmore's Lorna Doone.
Browning's Shorter Poems.
Browning, Mrs., Poems (Selected).
Bryant's Thanatopsis, etc.
Bulwer's Last Days of Pompeii.
Bunyan's The Pilgrim's Progress.
Burke's Speech on Conciliation.
Burns' Poems (Selections from).
Byron's Childe Harold's Pilgrimage.
Byron's Shorter Poems.
Carlyle's Essay on Burns.
Carlyle's Heroes and Hero Worship.
Carroll's Alice's Adventures in Wonderland (Illustrated).
Chaucer's Prologue and Knight's Tale.
Church's The Story of the Iliad.
Church's The Story of the Odyssey.
Coleridge's The Ancient Mariner.
Cooper's The Deerslayer.
Cooper's The Last of the Mohicans.
Cooper's The Spy.
Dana's Two Years Before the Mast.
Defoe's Robinson Crusoe.
De Quincey's Confessions of an English Opium-Eater.
De Quincey's Joan of Arc, and The English Mail-Coach.
Dickens' A Christmas Carol, and The Cricket on the Hearth.
Dickens' A Tale of Two Cities.
Dryden's Palamon and Arcite.
Early American Orations, 1760-1824.
Edwards' (Jonathan) Sermons.
Eliot's Silas Marner.

Emerson's Essays.
Emerson's Early Poems.
Emerson's Representative Men.
English Narrative Poems.
Epoch-making Papers in U. S. History.
Franklin's Autobiography.
Gaskell's Cranford.
Goldsmith's The Deserted Village, She Stoops to Conquer, and The Good-natured Man.
Goldsmith's The Vicar of Wakefield.
Gray's Elegy, etc., and Cowper's John Gilpin, etc.
Grimm's Fairy Tales.
Hawthorne's Grandfather's Chair.
Hawthorne's Mosses from an Old Manse.
Hawthorne's Tanglewood Tales.
Hawthorne's The House of the Seven Gables.
Hawthorne's Twice-told Tales (Selections from).
Hawthorne's Wonder-Book.
Holmes' Poems.
Homer's Iliad (Translated).
Homer's Odyssey (Translated).
Hughes' Tom Brown's School Days.
Huxley's Autobiography and Lay Sermons.
Irving's Life of Goldsmith.
Irving's Knickerbocker.
Irving's The Alhambra.
Irving's Sketch Book.
Irving's Tales of a Traveller.
Keary's Heroes of Asgard.
Kingsley's The Heroes.
Lamb's The Essays of Elia.
Lincoln's Inaugurals and Speeches.
Longfellow's Evangeline.
Longfellow's Hiawatha.
Longfellow's Miles Standish.

Macmillan's Pocket American and English Classics

A SERIES OF ENGLISH TEXTS, EDITED FOR USE IN ELEMENTARY AND
SECONDARY SCHOOLS, WITH CRITICAL INTRODUCTIONS, NOTES, ETC.

16mo   Cloth   25 cents each

Longfellow's Tales of a Wayside Inn.
Lowell's The Vision of Sir Launfal.
Macaulay's Essay on Addison.
Macaulay's Essay on Hastings.
Macaulay's Essay on Lord Clive.
Macaulay's Essay on Milton.
Macaulay's Lays of Ancient Rome.
Macaulay's Life of Samuel Johnson.
Milton's Comus and Other Poems.
Malory's Le Morte Darthur.
Milton's Paradise Lost, Books I. and II.
Old English Ballads.
Out of the Northland.
Palgrave's Golden Treasury.
Parkman's Oregon Trail.
Plutarch's Lives (Cæsar, Brutus, and
   Mark Antony).
Poe's Poems.
Poe's Prose Tales (Selections from).
Pope's Homer's Iliad.
Pope's The Rape of the Lock.
Ruskin's Sesame and Lilies.
Ruskin's Crown of Wild Olive and Queen
   of the Air.
Scott's Ivanhoe.
Scott's Kenilworth.
Scott's Lady of the Lake.
Scott's Lay of the Last Minstrel.
Scott's Marmion.
Scott's Quentin Durward.
Scott's The Talisman.
Shakespeare's As You Like It.
Shakespeare's Hamlet.
Shakespeare's Henry V.

Shakespeare's Julius Cæsar.
Shakespeare's King Lear.
Shakespeare's Macbeth.
Shakespeare's A Midsummer Night's
   Dream.
Shakespeare's Merchant of Venice.
Shakespeare's Richard II.
Shakespeare's The Tempest.
Shakespeare's Twelfth Night.
Shelley and Keats: Poems.
Sheridan's The Rivals and The School
   for Scandal.
Southern Poets: Selections.
Southern Orators: Selections.
Spenser's Faerie Queene, Book I.
Stevenson's Kidnapped.
Stevenson's The Master of Ballantrae.
Stevenson's Travels with a Donkey, and
   An Inland Voyage.
Stevenson's Treasure Island.
Swift's Gulliver's Travels.
Tennyson's Idylls of the King.
Tennyson's The Princess.
Tennyson's Shorter Poems.
Thackeray's English Humourists.
Thackeray's Henry Esmond.
Thoreau's Walden.
Virgil's Æneid.
Washington's Farewell Address, and
   Webster's First Bunker Hill Oration.
Whittier's Snow-Bound and Other Early
   Poems.
Woolman's Journal.
Wordsworth's Shorter Poems.

THE RIVALS

AND

THE SCHOOL FOR SCANDAL

BY

RICHARD BRINSLEY SHERIDAN

EDITED
WITH INTRODUCTION AND NOTES
BY

WILL DAVID HOWE, Ph.D.
DEPARTMENT OF ENGLISH, INDIANA UNIVERSITY

WILDSIDE PRESS

To
MY MOTHER

AUTHOR'S PREFACE

TO THE EDITION OF 1775

A PREFACE to a play seems generally to be considered as a kind of closet-prologue, in which — if
his piece has been successful — the author solicits
that indulgence from the reader which he had before
experienced from the audience: but as the scope
and immediate object of a play is to please a mixed
assembly in *representation* (whose judgment in the
theatre at least is decisive), its degree of reputation
is usually as determined as public, before it can be
prepared for the cooler tribunal of the study.   Thus
any farther solicitude on the part of the writer becomes unnecessary at least, if not an intrusion: and
if the piece has been condemned in the performance,
I fear an address to the closet, like an appeal to
posterity, is constantly regarded as the procrastina-
tion of a suit, from a consciousness of the weakness
of the cause.   From these considerations, the following comedy would certainly have been submitted
to the reader, without any farther introduction
than what it had in the representation, but that

its success has probably been founded on a circumstance which the author is informed has not before
attended a theatrical trial, and which consequently
ought not to pass unnoticed.

  I need scarcely add, that the circumstance alluded
to was the withdrawing of the piece,° to remove
those imperfections in the first representation which
were too obvious to escape reprehension, and too
numerous to admit of a hasty correction. There
are few writers, I believe, who, even in the fullest
consciousness of error, do not wish to palliate the
faults which they acknowledge; and, however
trifling the performance, •to second their confession
of its deficiencies, by whatever plea seems least dis-
graceful to their ability. In the present instance, it
cannot be said to amount either to candour or
modesty in me, to acknowledge an extreme inexperience and want of judgment on matters, in which,
without guidance from practice, or spur from success,
a young man should scarcely boast of being an
adept. If it be said, that under such disadvantages
no one should attempt to write a play, I must beg
leave to dissent from the position, while the first
point of experience that I have gained on the
subject is, a knowledge of the candour and judgment with which an impartial public distinguishes
between the errors of inexperience and incapacity,

and the indulgence which it shows even to a disposition to remedy the defects of either.

It were unnecessary to enter into any farther
extenuation of what was thought exceptionable in
this play, but that it has been said, that the managers
should have prevented some of the defects before
its appearance to the public — and in particular
the uncommon length of the piece as represented
the first night. It were an ill return for the most
liberal and gentlemanly conduct on their side, to
suffer any censure to rest where none was deserved.
Hurry in writing has long been exploded as an excuse
for an author; — however, in the dramatic line,
it may happen, that both an author and a manager
may wish to fill a chasm in the entertainment of
the public with a hastiness not altogether culpable.
The season was advanced when I first put the play
into Mr. Harris's° hands: it was at that time at
least double the length of any acting comedy. I
profited by his judgment and experience in the .
curtailing of it — till, I believe, his feeling for the
vanity of a young author got the better of his desire
for correctness, and he left many excrescences
remaining, because he had assisted in pruning so
many more. Hence, though I was not uninformed
that the acts were still too long, I flattered myself
that, after the first trial, I might with safer judg-

ment proceed to remove what should appear to have been most dissatisfactory. Many other errors there were, which might in part have arisen from my being by no means conversant with plays in general, either in reading or at the theatre. Yet I own that, in one respect, I did not regret my ignorance: for as my first wish in attempting a play was to avoid every appearance of plagiary, I thought I should stand a better chance of effecting this from being in a walk which I had not frequented, and where, consequently, the progress of invention was less likely to be interrupted by starts of recollection: for on subjects on which the mind has been much informed, invention is slow of exerting itself. Faded ideas float in the fancy like half-forgotten dreams; and the imagination in its fullest enjoyments becomes suspicious of its offspring, and doubts whether it has created or adopted.

With regard to some particular passages which on the first night's representation seemed generally disliked, I confess, that if I felt any emotion of surprise at the disapprobation, it was not that they were disapproved of, but that I had not before perceived that they deserved it. As some part of the attack on the piece was begun too early to pass for the sentence of *judgment*, which is ever tardy in condemning, it has been suggested to me, that much of the disapprobation must have arisen from virulence of malice, rather than severity of criticism: but as I was more apprehensive of there being just grounds to excite the latter than conscious of having deserved the former, I continue not to believe that probable, which I am sure must have been unprovoked. However, if it was so, and I could even mark the quarter from whence it came, it would be ungenerous to retort: for no passion suffers more than malice from disappointment. For my own part, I see no reason why the author of a play should not regard a first night's audience as a candid and judicious friend attending, in behalf of the public, at his last rehearsal. If he can dispense with flattery, he is sure at least of sincerity, and even though the annotation be rude, he may rely upon the justness of the comment. Considered in this light, that audience, whose *fiat* is essential to the poet's claim, whether his object be fame or profit, has surely a right to expect some deference to its opinion, from principles of politeness at least, if not from gratitude.

As for the little puny critics, who scatter their peevish strictures in private circles, and scribble at every author who has the eminence of being unconnected with them, as they are usually spleen-swoln from a vain idea of increasing their conse-

quence, there will always be found a petulance and
illiberality in their remarks, which should place
them as far beneath the notice of a gentleman, as
their original dulness had sunk them from the level
of the most unsuccessful author.

It is not without pleasure that I catch at an
opportunity of justifying myself from the charge
of intending any national reflection in the character
of Sir Lucius O'Trigger. If any gentleman opposed
the piece from that idea, I thank them sincerely
for their opposition; and if the condemnation of
this comedy (however misconceived the provocation) could have added one spark to the decaying
flame of national attachment to the country supposed to be reflected on, I should have been happy
in its fate; and might with truth have boasted,
that it had done more real service in its failure,
than the successful morality of a thousand stage-
novels will ever effect.

It is usual, I believe, to thank the performers in
a new play, for the exertion of their several abilities.
But where (as in this instance) their merit has been
so striking and uncontroverted, as to call for the
warmest and truest applause from a number of
judicious audiences, the poet's after-praise comes
like the feeble acclamation of a child to close the
shouts of a multitude. The conduct, however, of

the principals in a theatre cannot be so apparent
to the public. I think it therefore but justice to
declare, that from this theatre (the only one I can
speak of from experience) those writers who wish
to try the dramatic line will meet with that candour
and liberal attention, which are generally allowed
to be better calculated to lead genius into excellence,
than either the precepts of judgment, or the guidance
of experience.

THE AUTHOR.

THE RIVALS

DRAMATIS PERSONÆ

AS ORIGINALLY ACTED AT COVENT-GARDEN THEATRE IN 1775

SIR ANTHONY ABSOLUTE . .	Mr. Shuter.
CAPTAIN ABSOLUTE . . .	Mr. Woodward.
FAULKLAND	Mr. Lewis.
ACRES	Mr. Quick.
SIR LUCIUS O'TRIGGER . . .	Mr. Lee.
FAG	Mr. Lee Lewes.
DAVID	Mr. Dunstal.
THOMAS	Mr. Fearon.
MRS. MALAPROP	Mrs. Green.
LYDIA LANGUISH	Miss Barsanti.
JULIA	Mrs. Bulkley.
LUCY	Mrs. Lessingham.

Maid, Boy, Servants, &c.

SCENE: *Bath*

Time of Action — Five Hours

xxxii

THE SCHOOL FOR SCANDAL

DRAMATIS PERSONÆ

AS ORIGINALLY ACTED AT DRURY-LANE THEATRE° IN 1777

SIR PETER TEAZLE . . .	*Mr. King.*
SIR OLIVER SURFACE . . .	*Mr. Yates.*
SIR HARRY BUMPER . . .	*Mr. Gawdry.*
SIR BENJAMIN BACKBITE . .	*Mr. Dodd.*
JOSEPH SURFACE	*Mr. Palmer.*
CHARLES SURFACE . . .	*Mr. Smith.*
CARELESS	*Mr. Farren.*
SNAKE	*Mr. Packer.*
CRABTREE	*Mr. Parsons.*
ROWLEY	*Mr. Aickin.*
MOSES	*Mr. Baddeley.*
TRIP	*Mr. Lamask.*
LADY TEAZLE	*Mrs. Abington.*
LADY SNEERWELL . . .	*Miss Sherry.*
MRS. CANDOUR	*Miss Pope.*
MARIA	*Miss P. Hopkins.*

Gentlemen, Maid, and Servants

SCENE: *London*

xxxiii

THE RIVALS

A COMEDY

---◆◆◆---

PROLOGUE

BY THE AUTHOR

SPOKEN BY MR. WOODWARD AND MR. QUICK

Enter SERJEANT-AT-LAW *and* ATTORNEY *following
and giving a paper*

Serj. What's here! — a vile cramp hand! I
cannot see
Without my spectacles.
  Att.   He means his fee.
Nay, Mr. Serjeant, good sir, try again. [*Gives money.*
 Serj. The scrawl improves! [*more*] O come, 'tis
pretty plain.
Hey! how's this? Dibble! — sure it cannot be! 5
A poet's brief! a poet and a fee!
 Att. Yes, sir! though you without reward, I know,
Would gladly plead the Muse's cause.
 Serj.   So! — so!

B   1

Att. And if the fee offends, your wrath should fall
On me.
    Serj. Dear Dibble, no offence at all.
    Att. Some sons of Phœbus° in the courts we meet —
    Serj. And fifty sons of Phœbus in the Fleet°!
5   *Att.* Nor pleads he worse, who with a decent sprig
Of bays° adorns his legal waste of wig.
    Serj. Full-bottomed heroes thus, on signs, unfurl
A leaf of laurel in a grove of curl!
Yet tell your client, that, in adverse days,
10 This wig is warmer than a bush of bays.
    Att. Do you, then, sir, my client's place supply,
Profuse of robe, and prodigal of tie ——
Do you, with all those blushing powers of face,
And wonted bashful hesitating grace,
15 Rise in the court, and flourish on the case. [*Exit.*
    Serj. For practice then suppose — this brief will
    show it, —
Me, Serjeant Woodward, — counsel for the poet.
Used to the ground, I know 'tis hard to deal
With this dread court, from whence there's no
    appeal;
20 No tricking here, to blunt the edge of law,
Or, damned in equity, escape by flaw:
But judgment given, your sentence must remain;
No writ of error lies — to Drury-lane°:

Yet when so kind you seem, 'tis past dispute
We gain some favour, if not costs of suit.
No spleen is here! I see no hoarded fury; —
I think I never faced a milder jury!
Sad else our plight! where frowns are transporta-
    tion,   5
A hiss the gallows, and a groan damnation!
But such the public candour, without fear
My client waves all right of challenge here.
No newsman from our session is dismissed,
Nor wit nor critic we scratch off the list;   10
His faults can never hurt another's ease,
His crime, at worst, a bad attempt to please:
Thus, all respecting, he appeals to all,
And by the general voice will stand or fall.

PROLOGUE

BY THE AUTHOR

SPOKEN ON THE TENTH NIGHT, BY MRS. BULKLEY

Granted our cause, our suit and trial o'er,
The worthy serjeant need appear no more:
In pleasing I a different client choose,
He served the Poet — I would serve the Muse:
5 Like him, I'll try to merit your applause,
A female counsel in a female's cause.
   Look on this form,¹ — where humour, quaint
    and sly,
Dimples the cheek, and points the beaming eye;
Where gay invention seems to boast its wiles
10 In amorous hint, and half-triumphant smiles;
While her light mask or covers satire's strokes,
Or hides the conscious blush her wit provokes.
Look on her well — does she seem formed to teach?
Should you expect to hear this lady preach?
15 Is grey experience suited to her youth?
Do solemn sentiments become that mouth?
Bid her be grave, those lips should rebel prove
To every theme that slanders mirth or love.

¹ Pointing to the figure of Comedy.

4

Yet, thus adorned with every graceful art
To charm the fancy and yet reach the heart,
Must we displace her? And instead advance
The goddess of the woful countenance —
The sentimental Muse! — Her emblems view,   5
The Pilgrim's Progress, and a sprig of rue!
View her — too chaste to look like flesh and blood —
Primly portrayed on emblematic wood!
There, fixed in usurpation, should she stand,
She'll snatch the dagger from her sister's hand: 10
And having made her votaries weep a flood,
Good heaven! she'll end her comedies in blood —
Bid Harry Woodward break poor Dunstal's crown°!
Imprison Quick, and knock Ned Shuter down;
While sad Barsanti, weeping o'er the scene,   15
Shall stab herself — or poison Mrs. Green.
    Such dire encroachments to prevent in time,
Demands the critic's voice — the poet's rhyme.
Can our light scenes add strength to holy laws!
Such puny patronage but hurts the cause: 20
Fair virtue scorns our feeble aid to ask;
And moral truth disdains the trickster's mask.
For here their favourite stands,[1] whose brow severe
And sad, claims youth's respect, and pity's tear;
Who, when oppress'd by foes her worth creates,   25
Can point a poniard at the guilt she hates.

[1] Pointing to Tragedy.

ACT I

Scene I. *A Street*

Enter Thomas; *he crosses the Stage;* Fag *follows,*
looking after him

Fag. What! Thomas! sure 'tis he? — What!
Thomas! Thomas!

Thos. Hey! — Odd's° life! Mr. Fag! — give us
your hand, my old fellow-servant.

5   *Fag.* Excuse my glove, Thomas: — I'm devilish
glad to see you, my lad. Why, my prince of
charioteers, you look as hearty — but who the
deuce thought of seeing you in Bath?

Thos. Sure, master, Madam Julia, Harry, Mrs.
10 Kate, and the postillion, be all come.

Fag. Indeed!

Thos. Ay, master thought another fit of the gout
was coming to make him a visit; — so he'd a mind
to gi't the slip, and whip! we were all off at an
15 hour's warning.

Fag. Ay, ay, hasty in every thing, or it would not
be Sir Anthony Absolute!

6

Thos. But tell us, Mr. Fag, how does young master? Odd! Sir Anthony will stare to see the Captain here!

Fag. I do not serve Captain Absolute now.

Thos. Why sure!   5

Fag. At present I am employed by Ensign Beverley.

Thos. I doubt, Mr. Fag, you ha'n't changed for the better.

Fag. I have not changed, Thomas.   10

Thos. No! Why, didn't you say you had left young master?

Fag. No. — Well, honest Thomas, I must puzzle you no farther: — briefly then — Captain Absolute and Ensign Beverley are one and the same 15 person.

Thos. The devil they are!

Fag. So it is indeed, Thomas; and the ensign half of my master being on guard at present — the captain has nothing to do with me.   20

Thos. So, so! — What, this is some freak, I warrant! — Do tell us, Mr. Fag, the meaning o't — you know I ha' trusted you.

Fag. You'll be secret, Thomas?

Thos. As a coach-horse.   25

Fag. Why then the cause of all this is — Love, —

Love, Thomas, who, (as you may get read to you,) has been a masquerader ever since the days of Jupiter.

Thos. Ay, ay; — I guessed there was a lady in
5 the case: — but pray, why does your master pass only for ensign? — Now if he had shammed general indeed ——

Fag. Ah! Thomas, there lies the mystery o' the matter. Hark'ee, Thomas, my master is in love
10 with a lady of a very singular taste: a lady who likes him better as a half pay ensign than if she knew he was son and heir to Sir Anthony Absolute, a baronet of three thousand a year.

Thos. That is an odd taste indeed! — But has
15 she got the stuff, Mr. Fag? Is she rich, hey?

Fag. Rich! — Why, I believe she owns half the stocks! Zounds°! Thomas, she could pay the national debt as easily as I could my washer-woman! She has a lapdog that eats out of gold, — she
20 feeds her parrot with small pearls, — and all her thread-papers° are made of bank-notes.

Thos. Bravo, faith! — Odd! I warrant she has a set of thousands° at least: — but does she draw kindly with the captain?

25   *Fag.* As fond as pigeons.

Thos. May one hear her name?

Fag. Miss Lydia Languish. — But there is an old tough aunt in the way; though, by the by, she has never seen my master — for we got acquainted with miss while on a visit in Gloucestershire.

Thos. Well — I wish they were once harnessed 5 together in matrimony. — But pray, Mr. Fag, what kind of a place is this Bath? — I ha' heard a deal of it — here's a mort o' merry-making,° hey?

Fag. Pretty well, Thomas, pretty well — 'tis a 10 good lounge; in the morning we go to the pump-room° (though neither my master nor I drink the waters); after breakfast we saunter on the parades, or play a game at billiards; at night we dance; but I'm tired of the place: their regular hours 15 stupify me — not a fiddle nor a card after eleven! — However, Mr. Faulkland's gentleman and I keep it up a little in private parties; — I'll introduce you there, Thomas — you'll like him much.

Thos. Sure I know Mr. Du-Peigne — you know 20 his master is to marry Madam Julia.

Fag. I had forgot. — But, Thomas, you must polish a little — indeed you must. — Here now — this wig! — What the devil do you do with a wig,° Thomas? — None of the London whips of any degree 25 of *ton*° wear wigs now.

Thos. More's the pity! more's the pity, I say. — Odd's life! when I heard how the lawyers and doctors had took to their own hair, I thought how 'twould go next: — odd rabbit it! when the
5 fashion had got foot on the bar, I guessed 'twould mount to the box! — but 'tis all out of character, believe me, Mr. Fag: and look'ee, I'll never gi' up mine — the lawyers and doctors may do as they will.

10 *Fag.* Well, Thomas, we'll not quarrel about that.

Thos. Why, bless you, the gentlemen of the professions ben't all of a mind — for in our village now, thoff° Jack Gauge, the exciseman, has ta'en
15 to his carrots,° there's little Dick the farrier swears he'll never forsake his bob,° though all the college should appear with their own heads!

Fag. Indeed! well said, Dick! — But hold — mark! mark! Thomas.

20 *Thos.* Zooks°! 'tis the captain. — Is that the lady with him?

Fag. No, no, that is Madam Lucy, my master's mistress's maid. They lodge at that house — but I must after him to tell him the news.

25 *Thos.* Odd! he's giving her money! — Well, Mr. Fag ——

Fag. Good-bye, Thomas. I have an appointment in Gyde's Porch° this evening at eight; meet me there, and we'll make a little party.

[*Exeunt severally.*

SCENE II. *A Dressing-room in Mrs. Malaprop's Lodgings*

LYDIA *sitting on a sofa, with a book in her hand.*
        LUCY, *as just returned from a message*

Lucy. Indeed, ma'am, I traversed half the town in search of it: I don't believe there's a circulating 5 library° in Bath I ha'n't been at.

Lyd. And could not you get *The Reward of Constancy?*

Lucy. No, indeed, ma'am.

Lyd. Nor *The Fatal Connection?*   10

Lucy. No, indeed, ma'am.

Lyd. Nor *The Mistakes of the Heart?*

Lucy. Ma'am, as ill luck would have it, Mr. Bull said Miss Sukey Saunter had just fetched it away.

Lyd. Heigh-ho! — Did you inquire for *The Deli-* 15 *cate Distress?*

Lucy. Or, *The Memoirs of Lady Woodford?* Yes, indeed, ma'am. I asked everywhere for it; and I might have brought it from Mr. Frederick's, but Lady Slattern Lounger, who had just sent it home, had so soiled and dog's-eared it, it wa'n't fit for a Christian to read.

Lyd. Heigh-ho! — Yes, I always know when ₅ Lady Slattern has been before me. She has a most observing thumb; and, I believe, cherishes her nails for the convenience of making marginal notes. — Well, child, what have you brought me?

Lucy. Oh! here, ma'am. — [*Taking books from* ₁₀ *under her cloak, and from her pockets.*] This is *The Gordian Knot,* — and this *Peregrine Pickle.* Here are *The Tears of Sensibility,* and *Humphrey Clinker.* This is *The Memoirs of a Lady of Quality, written by herself,* and here the second volume of *The Senti-* ₁₅ *mental Journey.*

Lyd. Heigh-ho! — What are those books by the glass?

Lucy. The great one is only *The Whole Duty of Man,* where I press a few blonds,° ma'am.

₂₀ *Lyd.* Very well — give me the sal volatile.°

Lucy. Is it in a blue cover, ma'am?

Lyd. My smelling-bottle, you simpleton!

Lucy. Oh, the drops! — here, ma'am.

Lyd. Hold! — here's some one coming — quick, ₂₅ see who it is. — [*Exit* LUCY.] Surely I heard my cousin Julia's voice.

Reënter LUCY

Lucy. Lud! ma'am, here is Miss Melville.
Lyd. Is it possible! —   [*Exit* LUCY.

· *Enter* JULIA

Lyd. My dearest Julia, how delighted am I! —
[*Embrace.*] How unexpected was this happiness!
Jul. True, Lydia — and our pleasure is the 5
greater. — But what has been the matter? — you
were denied to me at first!
Lyd. Ah, Julia, I have a thousand things to tell
you! — But first inform me what has conjured
you to Bath? — Is Sir Anthony here?   .   10
Jul. He is — we are arrived within this hour!
— and I suppose he will be here to wait on Mrs.
Malaprop as soon as he is dressed.
Lyd. Then before we are interrupted, let me im-
part to you some of my distress! — I know your 15
gentle nature will sympathize with me, though
your prudence may condemn me! My letters
have informed you of my whole connection with
Beverley; but I have lost him, Julia! My aunt
has discovered our intercourse by a note she inter- 20
cepted, and has confined me ever since! Yet, ·

would you believe it? she has absolutely fallen in love with a tall Irish baronet she met one night since we have been here, at Lady Macshuffle's rout.°

Jul. You jest, Lydia!

5 *Lyd.* No, upon my word. — She really carries on a kind of correspondence with him, under a feigned name though, till she chooses to be known to him; — but it is a Delia or a Celia, I assure you.

Jul. Then, surely, she is now more indulgent to 10 her niece.

Lyd. Quite the contrary. Since she has discovered her own frailty, she is become more suspicious of mine. Then I must inform you of another plague! — That odious Acres is to be in Bath 15 to-day; so that I protest I shall be teased out of all spirits!

Jul. Come, come, Lydia, hope for the best — Sir Anthony shall use his interest with Mrs. Malaprop.

20 *Lyd.* But you have not heard the worst. Unfortunately I had quarrelled with my poor Beverley, just before my aunt made the discovery, and I have not seen him since, to make it up.

Jul. What was his offence?

25 *Lyd.* Nothing at all! — But, I don't know how ˙it was, as often as we had been together, we had

never had a quarrel, and, somehow, I was afraid he
would never give me an opportunity. So, last
Thursday, I wrote a letter to myself, to inform
myself that Beverley was at that time paying his
addresses to another woman. I signed it *your* 5
friend unknown, showed it to Beverley, charged him
with his falsehood, put myself in a violent passion,
and vowed I'd never see him more.

Jul. And you let him depart so, and have not
seen him since?   10

Lyd. 'Twas the next day my aunt found the matter out. I intended only to have teased him three
days and a half, and now I've lost him for ever.

Jul. If he is as deserving and sincere as you have
represented him to me, he will never give you up 15
so. Yet consider, Lydia, you tell me he is but an
ensign, and you have thirty thousand pounds.

Lyd. But you know I lose most of my fortune if
I marry without my aunt's consent, till of age;
and that is what I have determined to do, ever 20
since I knew the penalty. Nor could I love the
man who would wish to wait a day for the alterna-
tive.

Jul. Nay, this is caprice!

Lyd. What, does Julia tax me with caprice? — 25
I thought her lover Faulkland had inured her to it.

Jul. I do not love even his faults.

Lyd. But apropos — you have sent to him, I suppose?

Jul. Not yet, upon my word — nor has he the
5 least idea of my being in Bath. Sir Anthony's resolution was so sudden, I could not inform him of it.

Lyd. Well, Julia, you are your own mistress, (though under the protection of Sir Anthony,)
10 yet have you, for this long year, been a slave to the caprice, the whim, the jealousy of this ungrateful Faulkland, who will ever delay assuming the right of a husband, while you suffer him to be equally imperious as a lover.

15 *Jul.* Nay, you are wrong entirely. We were contracted before my father's death. That, and some consequent embarrassments, have delayed what I know to be my Faulkland's most ardent wish. He is too generous to trifle on such a point:
20 — and for his character, you wrong him there too. No, Lydia, he is too proud, too noble to be jealous; if he is captious, 'tis without dissembling; if fretful, without rudeness. Unused to the fopperies of love, he is negligent of the little duties expected
25 from a lover — but being unhackneyed in the passion, his affection is ardent and sincere; and as

it engrosses his whole soul, he expects every thought
and emotion of his mistress to move in unison with
his. Yet, though his pride calls for this full return,
his humility makes him undervalue those qualities
in him which would entitle him to it; and not 5
feeling why he should be loved to the degree he
wishes, he still suspects that he is not loved enough.
This temper, I must own, has cost me many unhappy hours; but I have learned to think myself
his debtor, for those imperfections which arise from 10
the ardour of his attachment.

Lyd. Well, I cannot blame you for defending
him. But tell me candidly, Julia, had he never
saved your life, do you think you should have been
attached to him as you are? — Believe me, the 15
rude blast that overset your boat was a prosperous
gale of love to him.

Jul. Gratitude may have strengthened my attachment to Mr. Faulkland, but I loved him before
he had preserved me; yet surely that alone were an 20
obligation sufficient.

Lyd. Obligation! why a water spaniel would
have done as much! — Well, I should never think
of giving my heart to a man because he could swim.

Jul. Come, Lydia, you are too inconsiderate. 25

Lyd. Nay, I do but jest. — What's here?

c

Reënter Lucy *in a hurry*

Lucy. O ma'am, here is Sir Anthony Absolute just come home with your aunt.

Lyd. They'll not come here. — Lucy, do you watch.   [*Exit* Lucy.

5 *Jul.* Yet I must go. Sir Anthony does not know I am here, and if we meet, he'll detain me, to show me the town. I'll take another opportunity of paying my respects to Mrs. Malaprop, when she shall treat me, as long as she chooses, with her 10 select words so ingeniously misapplied, without being mispronounced.

Reënter Lucy

Lucy. O Lud°! ma'am, they are both coming upstairs.

Lyd. Well, I'll not detain you, coz.° — Adieu, 15 my dear Julia, I'm sure you are in haste to send to Faulkland. — There — through my room you'll find another staircase.

Jul. Adieu!   [*Embraces* Lydia *and exit.*

Lyd. Here, my dear Lucy, hide these books. 20 Quick, quick. — Fling *Peregrine Pickle* under the toilet — throw *Roderick Random* into the closet —

put *The Innocent Adultery* into *The Whole Duty of
Man* — thrust *Lord Aimworth* under the sofa —
cram *Ovid* behind the bolster — there — put *The
Man of Feeling* into your pocket — so, so — now
lay *Mrs. Chapone* in sight, and leave *Fordyce's* 5
Sermons open on the table.

Lucy. O burn it, ma'am! the hairdresser has
torn away as far as *Proper Pride*.

Lyd. Never mind — open at *Sobriety*. — Fling
me *Lord Chesterfield's Letters*. — Now for 'em.   10
                                      [*Exit* Lucy.

Enter Mrs. Malaprop, *and* Sir Anthony Absolute

Mrs. Mal. There, Sir Anthony, there sits the de-
liberate simpleton who wants to disgrace her family,
and lavish herself on a fellow not worth a shilling.

Lyd. Madam, I thought you once ——

Mrs. Mal. You thought, miss! I don't know 15
any business you have to think at all — thought
does not become a young woman. But the point
we would request of you is, that you will promise
to forget this fellow — to illiterate° him, I say,
quite from your memory.   20

Lyd. Ah, madam! our memories are independent of our wills. It is not so easy to forget.

Mrs. Mal. But I say it is, miss; there is nothing
on earth so easy as to forget, if a person chooses
to set about it. I'm sure I have as much forgot
your poor dear uncle as if he had never existed —
5 and I thought it my duty so to do; and let me tell
you, Lydia, these violent memories don't become a
young woman.

Sir Anth. Why sure she won't pretend to remember what she's ordered not! — ay, this comes
10 of her reading!

Lyd. What crime, madam, have I committed,
to be treated thus?

Mrs. Mal. Now don't attempt to extirpate°
yourself from the matter; you know I have proof
15 controvertible° of it. — But tell me, will you promise to do as you're bid? Will you take a husband
of your friends' choosing?

Lyd. Madam, I must tell you plainly, that had I
no preference for any one else, the choice you have
20 made would be my aversion.

Mrs. Mal. What business have you, miss, with
preference and aversion? They don't become a
young woman; and you ought to know, that as
both always wear off, 'tis safest in matrimony to
25 begin with a little aversion. I am sure I hated your
poor dear uncle before marriage as if he had been a

blackamoor — and yet, miss, you are sensible what
a wife I made! — and when it pleased Heaven
to release me from him, 'tis unknown what tears
I shed! — But suppose we were going to give you
another choice, will you promise us to give up this 5
Beverley?

Lyd. Could I belie my thoughts so far as to give
that promise, my actions would certainly as far
belie my words.

Mrs. Mal. Take yourself to your room. — You 10
are fit company for nothing but your own ill-
humours.

Lyd. Willingly, ma'am — I cannot change for
the worse.   [*Exit.*

Mrs. Mal. There's a little intricate° hussy for 15
you!

Sir Anth. It is not to be wondered at, ma'am, —
all this is the natural consequence of teaching girls
to read. Had I a thousand daughters, by Heaven!
I'd as soon have them taught the black art° as their 20
alphabet!

Mrs. Mal. Nay, nay, Sir Anthony, you are an
absolute misanthropy.°

Sir Anth. In my way hither, Mrs. Malaprop, I
observed your niece's maid coming forth from a 25
circulating library! — She had a book in each hand

— they were half-bound volumes, with marble
covers! — From that moment I guessed how full
of duty I should see her mistress!

   Mrs. Mal. Those are vile places, indeed!

5   *Sir Anth.* Madam, a circulating library in a town
is as an evergreen tree of diabolical knowledge!
It blossoms through the year! — And depend on
it, Mrs. Malaprop, that they who are so fond of
handling the leaves, will long for the fruit at last.

10   *Mrs. Mal.* Fy, fy, Sir Anthony! you surely speak
laconically.°

   Sir Anth. Why, Mrs. Malaprop, in moderation
now, what would you have a woman know?

   Mrs. Mal. Observe me, Sir Anthony. I would
15 by no means wish a daughter of mine to be a
progeny° of learning; I don't think so much learning becomes a young woman: for instance, I would
never let her meddle with Greek, or Hebrew, or
algebra, or simony, or fluxions, or paradoxes, or
20 such inflammatory branches of learning — neither
would it be necessary for her to handle any of your
mathematical, astronomical, diabolical instruments.
— But, Sir Anthony, I would send her, at nine years
old, to a boarding-school, in order to learn a little
25 ingenuity° and artifice. Then, sir, she should have
a supercilious° knowledge in accounts; — and as

she grew up, I would have her instructed in geome-
try, that she might know something of the con-
tagious° countries; — but above all, Sir Anthony,
she should be mistress of orthodoxy,° that she might
not mis-spell, and mis-pronounce words so shame- 5
fully as girls usually do; and likewise that she might
reprehend° the true meaning of what she is saying.
This, Sir Anthony, is what I would have a woman
know; — and I don't think there is a superstitious°
article in it.   10

Sir Anth. Well, well, Mrs. Malaprop, I will dispute the point no further with you; though I must
confess, that you are a truly moderate and polite
arguer, for almost every third word you say is on
my side of the question. But, Mrs. Malaprop, to 15
the more important point in debate — you say
you have no objection to my proposal?

Mrs. Mal. None, I assure you. I am under no
positive engagement with Mr. Acres, and as Lydia
is so obstinate against him, perhaps your son may 20
have better success.

Sir Anth. Well, madam, I will write for the
boy directly. He knows not a syllable of this
yet, though I have for some time had the proposal in my head. He is at present with his regi- 25
ment.

Mrs. Mal. We have never seen your son, Sir
Anthony; bùt I hope no objection on his side.

Sir Anth. Objection! — let him object if he dare!
— No, no, Mrs. Malaprop, Jack knows that the least
5 demur puts me in a frenzy directly. My process
was always very simple — in their younger days,
'twas " Jack, do this;'' — if he demurred, I knocked
him down — and if he grumbled at that, I always
sent him out of the room.

10 *Mrs. Mal.* Ay, and the properest way, o' my
conscience! — nothing is so conciliating to young
people as severity. — Well, Sir Anthony, I shall give
Mr. Acres his discharge, and prepare Lydia to
receive your son's invocations; — and I hope you
15 will represent her to the captain as an object not
altogether illegible.°

Sir Anth. Madam, I will handle the subject
prudently. — Well, I must leave you; and let me
beg you, Mrs. Malaprop, to enforce this matter
20 roundly to the girl. — Take my advice — keep
a tight hand: if she rejects this proposal, clap
her under lock and key; and if you were just
to let the servants forget to bring her dinner for
three or four days, you can't conceive how she'd
25 come about.   [*Exit.*

Mrs. Mal. Well, at any rate I shall be glad to

get her from under my intuition.° She has somehow
discovered my partiality for Sir Lucius O'Trigger —
sure, Lucy can't have betrayed me! — No, the girl
is such a simpleton, I should have made her confess
it. — Lucy! — Lucy! — [*Calls.*] Had she been one of 5
your artificial ones, I should never have trusted her.

Reënter LUCY

Lucy. Did you call, ma'am?

Mrs. Mal. Yes, girl. — Did you see Sir Lucius
while you was out?

Lucy. No, indeed, ma'am, not a glimpse of him. 10

Mrs. Mal. You are sure, Lucy, that you never
mentioned —

Lucy. Oh gemini! I'd sooner cut my tongue out.

Mrs. Mal. Well, don't let your simplicity be
imposed on.   15

Lucy. No, ma'am.

Mrs. Mal. So, come to me presently, and I'll
give you another letter to Sir Lucius; but mind,
Lucy — if ever you betray what you are entrusted
with (unless it be other people's secrets to me), 20
you forfeit my malevolence° for ever; and your
being a simpleton shall be no excuse for your
locality.°   [*Exit.*

Lucy. Ha! ha! ha! — So, my dear Simplicity,

let me give you a little respite. — [*Altering her manner.*] Let girls in my station be as fond as they please of appearing expert and knowing in their trusts; commend me to a mask of silliness, and a
5 pair of sharp eyes for my own interest under it! — Let me see to what account have I turned my simplicity lately. — [*Looks at a paper.*] For *abetting Miss Lydia Languish in a design of running away with an ensign! — in money, sundry times, twelve*
10 *pound twelve; gowns, five; hats, ruffles, caps, &c. &c., numberless! — From the said ensign, within this last month, six guineas and a half.* — About a quarter's pay! — Item, *from Mrs. Malaprop, for betraying the young people to her* — when I found
15 matters were likely to be discovered — *two guineas, and a black paduasoy.*° — Item, *from Mr. Acres, for carrying divers letters* — which I never delivered — *two guineas, and a pair of buckles.* — Item, *from Sir Lucius O'Trigger, three crowns, two gold pocket-*
20 *pieces, and a silver snuff-box!* — Well done, Simplicity! — Yet I was forced to make my Hibernian believe, that he was corresponding, not with the aunt, but with the niece: for though not over rich, I found he had too much pride and delicacy to
25 sacrifice the feelings of a gentleman to the necessities of his fortune.   [*Exit.*

ACT II

SCENE I. *Captain Absolute's Lodgings*

CAPTAIN ABSOLUTE *and* FAG

Fag. Sir, while I was there Sir Anthony came in:
I told him, you had sent me to inquire after his
health, and to know if he was at leisure to see
you.

Abs. And what did he say, on hearing I was at 5
Bath?

Fag. Sir, in my life I never saw an elderly gentleman more astonished! He started back two or
three paces, rapped out a dozen interjectural oaths,
and asked, what the devil had brought you here. 10

Abs. Well, sir, and what did you say?

Fag. Oh, I lied, sir — I forget the precise lie;
but you may depend on't, he got no truth from me.
Yet, with submission, for fear of blunders in future,
I should be glad to fix what has brought us to Bath; 15
in order that we may lie a little consistently. Sir
Anthony's servants were curious, sir, very curious
indeed.

Abs. You have said nothing to them?

27

Fag. Oh, not a word, sir, — not a word! Mr.
Thomas, indeed, the coachman (whom I take to
be the discreetest of whips) ——

Abs. 'Sdeath! — you rascal! you have not
5 trusted him!

Fag. Oh, no, sir — no — no — not a syllable,
upon my veracity! — He was, indeed, a little inquisitive; but I was sly, sir — devilish sly! My
master (said I), honest Thomas (you know, sir,
10 one says honest to one's inferiors,) is come to Bath
to recruit — Yes, sir, I said to recruit — and whether
for men, money, or constitution, you know, sir, is
nothing to him, nor any one else.

Abs. Well, recruit will do — let it be so.

15 *Fag.* Oh, sir, recruit will do surprisingly —
indeed, to give the thing an air, I told Thomas, that
your honour had already enlisted five disbanded
chairmen,° seven minority waiters,° and thirteen
billiard-markers.

20 *Abs.* You blockhead, never say more than is
necessary.

Fag. I beg pardon, sir — I beg pardon — but,
with submission, a lie is nothing unless one supports
it. Sir, whenever I draw on my invention for a
25 good current lie, I always forge indorsements as
well as the bill.

Abs. Well, take care you don't hurt your credit, by offering too much security. — Is Mr. Faulkland returned?

Fag. He is above, sir, changing his dress.

Abs. Can you tell whether he has been informed of 5 Sir Anthony and Miss Melville's arrival?

Fag. I fancy not, sir; he has seen no one since he came in but his gentleman, who was with him at Bristol. — I think, sir, I hear Mr. Faulkland coming down —— 10

Abs. Go, tell him I am here.

Fag. Yes, sir. — [*Going.*]   I beg pardon, sir, but should Sir Anthony call, you will do me the favour to remember that we are recruiting, if you please.

Abs. Well, well. 15

Fag. And, in tenderness to my character, if your honour could bring in the chairmen and waiters, I should esteem it as an obligation; for though I never scruple a lie to serve my master, yet it hurts one's conscience to be found out.   [*Exit.* 20

Abs. Now for my whimsical friend — if he does not know that his mistress is here, I'll tease him a little before I tell him —

Enter FAULKLAND

Faulkland, you're welcome to Bath again; you are punctual in your return. 25

Faulk. Yes; I had nothing to detain me, when I had finished the business I went on. Well, what news since I left you? how stand matters between you and Lydia?

5 *Abs.* Faith, much as they were; I have not seen her since our quarrel; however, I expect to be recalled every hour.

Faulk. Why don't you persuade her to go off with you at once?

10 *Abs.* What, and lose two-thirds of her fortune? you forget that, my friend. — No, no, I could have brought her to that long ago.

Faulk. Nay then, you trifle too long — if you are sure of her, propose to the aunt in your own 15 character, and write to Sir Anthony for his consent.

Abs. Softly, softly; for though I am convinced my little Lydia would elope with me as Ensign Beverley, yet am I by no means certain that she 20 would take me with the impediment of our friends' consent, a regular humdrum wedding, and the reversion° of a good fortune on my side: no, no; I must prepare her gradually for the discovery, and make myself necessary to her, before I risk it. — 25 Well, but, Faulkland, you'll dine with us to-day at the hotel?

Faulk. Indeed I cannot; I am not in spirits to be of such a party.

Abs. By Heavens! I shall forswear your company. You are the most teasing, captious, incorrigible lover! — Do love like a man.   5

Faulk. I own I am unfit for company.

Abs. Am not I a lover; ay, and a romantic one too? Yet do I carry every where with me such a confounded farrago of doubts, fears, hopes, wishes, and all the flimsy furniture of a country miss's 10 brain?

Faulk. Ah! Jack, your heart and soul are not, like mine, fixed immutably on one only object. You throw for a large stake, but losing, you could stake and throw again: — but I have set my sum 15 of happiness on this cast, and not to succeed, were to be stripped of all.

Abs. But, for Heaven's sake! what grounds for apprehension can your whimsical brain conjure up at present?   20

Faulk. What grounds for apprehension, did you say? Heavens! are there not a thousand! I fear for her spirits — her health — her life. — My absence may fret her; her anxiety for my return, her fears for me may oppress her gentle temper: 25 and for her health, does not every hour bring me

cause to be alarmed? If it rains, some shower may
even then have chilled her delicate frame! If the
wind be keen, some rude blast may have affected her!
The heat of noon, the dews of the evening, may en-
5 danger the life of her, for whom only I value mine.
O Jack! when delicate and feeling souls are separated,
there is not a feature in the sky, not a movement of
the elements, not an aspiration of the breeze, but
hints some cause for a lover's apprehension!

10   *Abs.* Ay, but we may choose whether we will take
the hint or not. — So, then, Faulkland, if you were
convinced that Julia were well and in spirits, you
would be entirely content?

Faulk. I should be happy beyond measure — I
15 am anxious only for that.

Abs. Then to cure your anxiety at once — Miss
Melville is in perfect health, and is at this moment in
Bath.

Faulk. Nay, Jack — don't trifle with me.

20   *Abs.* She is arrived here with my father within
this hour.

Faulk. Can you be serious?

Abs. I thought you knew Sir Anthony better
than to be surprised at a sudden whim of this kind.
25 — Seriously, then, it is as I tell you — upon my
honour.

Faulk. My dear friend! — Hollo, Du-Peigne! my
hat. — My dear Jack — now nothing on earth can
give me a moment's uneasiness.

Reënter FAG

Fag. Sir, Mr. Acres, just arrived, is below.

Abs. Stay, Faulkland, this Acres lives within a 5
mile of Sir Anthony, and he shall tell you how your
mistress has been ever since you left her. — Fag,
show the gentleman up.   [*Exit* FAG.

Faulk. What, is he much acquainted in the
family?   10

Abs. Oh, very intimate: I insist on your not
going: besides, his character will divert you.

Faulk. Well, I should like to ask him a few
questions.

Abs. He is likewise a rival of mine — that is, of 15
my other self's, for he does not think his friend
Captain Absolute ever saw the lady in question;
and it is ridiculous enough to hear him complain
to me of one Beverley, a concealed skulking rival,
who ——   20

Faulk. Hush! — he's here.

D

Enter ACRES

Acres. Ha! my dear friend, noble captain, and
honest Jack, how do'st thou? just arrived, faith, as
you see. — Sir, your humble servant. — Warm work
on the roads, Jack! — Odds whips and wheels!
5 I've travelled like a comet, with a tail of dust all the
way as long as the Mall.°

Abs. Ah! Bob, you are indeed an eccentric planet,
but we know your attraction hither. — Give me leave
to introduce Mr. Faulkland to you; Mr. Faulkland,
10 Mr. Acres.

Acres. Sir, I am most heartily glad to see you:
sir, I solicit your connections. — Hey, Jack — what,
this is Mr. Faulkland, who ——

Abs. Ay, Bob, Miss Melville's Mr. Faulkland.

15 *Acres.* Odso! she and your father can be but
just arrived before me: — I suppose you have seen
them. Ah! Mr. Faulkland, you are indeed a happy
man.

Faulk. I have not seen Miss Melville yet, sir; —
20 I hope she enjoyed full health and spirits in Devonshire?

Acres. Never knew her better in my life, sir, —
never better. Odds blushes and blooms! she has
been as healthy as the German Spa.°

Faulk. Indeed! — I did hear that she had been a little indisposed.

Acres. False, false, sir — only said to vex you: quite the reverse, I assure you.

Faulk. There, Jack, you see she has the advantage 5 of me; I had almost fretted myself ill.

Abs. Now are you angry with your mistress for not having been sick?

Faulk. No, no, you misunderstand me: yet surely a little trifling indisposition is not an unnatural con- 10 sequence of absence from those we love. — Now confess — isn't there something unkind in this violent, robust, unfeeling health?

Abs. Oh, it was very unkind of her to be well in your absence, to be sure!   15

Acres. Good apartments, Jack.

Faulk. Well, sir, but you was saying that Miss Melville has been so exceedingly well — what, then, she has been merry and gay, I suppose? — Always in spirits — hey?   20

Acres. Merry, odds crickets! she has been the belle and spirit of the company wherever she has been — so lively and entertaining! so full of wit and humour!

Faulk. There, Jack, there. — Oh, by my soul! 25 there is an innate levity in woman, that nothing can overcome. — What! happy, and I away!

Abs. Have done. — How foolish this is! just now you were only apprehensive for your mistress' spirits.

Faulk. Why, Jack, have I been the joy and spirit 5 of the company?

Abs. No indeed, you have not.

Faulk. Have I been lively and entertaining?

Abs. Oh, upon my word, I acquit you.

Faulk. Have I been full of wit and humour?

10　　*Abs.* No, faith, to do you justice, you have been confoundedly stupid indeed.

Acres. What's the matter with the gentleman?

Abs. He is only expressing his great satisfaction at hearing that Julia has been so well and happy — 15 that's all — hey, Faulkland?

Faulk. Oh! I am rejoiced to hear it — yes, yes, she has a happy disposition!

Acres. That she has indeed. — Then she is so accomplished — so sweet a voice — so expert at her 20 harpsichord — such a mistress of flat and sharp, squallante, rumblante, and quiverante! — There was this time month — odds minims and cro chets! how she did chirrup at Mrs. Piano's concert!

Faulk. There again, what say you to this? You 25 see she has been all mirth and song — not a thought of me!

Abs. Pho! man, is not music the food of love?

Faulk. Well, well, it may be so. — Pray, Mr.
——, what's his name? — Do you remember what
songs Miss Melville sung?

Acres. Not I indeed.   5

Abs. Stay, now, they were some pretty melancholy purling-stream airs, I warrant; perhaps you
may recollect; — did she sing, *When absent from my
soul's delight?*

Acres. No, that wa'n't it.   10

Abs. Or, *Go, gentle gales!*   [*Sings.*

Acres. Oh, no! nothing like it. Odds! now I
recollect one of them — *My heart's my own, my will
is free.*   [*Sings.*

Faulk. Fool! fool that I am! to fix all my happi- 15
ness on such a trifler! 'Sdeath! to make herself the
pipe and balladmonger of a circle! to soothe her
light heart with catches° and glees! — What can
you say to this, sir?

Abs. Why, that I should be glad to hear my mis- 20
tress had been so merry, sir.

Faulk. Nay, nay, nay — I'm not sorry that she
has been happy — no, no, I am glad of that — I
would not have had her sad or sick — yet surely a
sympathetic heart would have shown itself even in 25
the choice of a song — she might have been tem-

perately healthy, and somehow, plaintively gay; —
but she has been dancing too, I doubt not!

Acres. What does the gentleman say about dancing?

5   *Abs.* He says the lady we speak of dances as well
as she sings.

Acres. Ay, truly, does she — there was at our
last race ball ——   .

Faulk. There! — there — I told you so! I told
10 you so! Oh! she thrives in my absence! — Dancing!
but her whole feelings have been in opposition with
mine; — I have been anxious, silent, pensive,
sedentary — my days have been hours of care, my
nights of watchfulness. — She has been all health!
15 spirit! laugh! song! dance! —

Abs. For Heaven's sake, Faulkland, don't expose yourself so! — Suppose she has danced, what
then? — does not the ceremony of society often
oblige ——

20   *Faulk.* Well, well, I'll contain myself — perhaps
as you say — for form sake. — What, Mr. Acres,
you were praising Miss Melville's manner of dancing
a minuet — hey?

Acres. Oh, I dare insure her for that — but what
25 I was going to speak of was her country-dancing.
Odds swimmings! she has such an air with her!

Faulk. Now disappointment on her! — Defend
this, Absolute; why don't you defend this? —
Country-dances! jigs and reels! am I to blame now?
A minuet I could have forgiven — I should not have
minded that — I say I should not have regarded 5
a minuet — but country-dances! — Zounds! had
she made one in a cotillon — I believe I could have
forgiven even that — but to be monkey-led for a
night! — to run the gauntlet through a string of
amorous palming puppies! — to show paces like 10
a managed filly! — Oh, Jack, there never can be but
one man in the world whom a truly modest and
delicate woman ought to pair with in a country-
dance; and, even then, the rest of the couples should
be her great-uncles and aunts!   15

Abs. Ay, to be sure! — grandfathers and grandmothers!

Faulk. If there be but one vicious mind in the set,
'twill spread like a contagion — the action of their
pulse beats to the lascivious movement of the jig — 20
their quivering, warm-breathed sighs impregnate
the very air — the atmosphere becomes electrical
to love, and each amorous spark darts through every
link of the chain! — I must leave you — I own I
am somewhat flurried — and that confounded looby° 25
has perceived it.   [*Going.*

Abs. Nay, but stay, Faulkland, and thank Mr. Acres for his good news.

Faulk. Damn his news!   [*Exit.*

Abs. Ha! ha! ha! poor Faulkland five minutes
5 since — "nothing on earth could give him a moment's uneasiness!"

Acres. The gentleman wa'n't angry at my praising his mistress, was he?

Abs. A little jealous, I believe, Bob.

10 *Acres.* You don't say so? Ha! ha! jealous of me — that's a good joke.

Abs. There's nothing strange in that, Bob; let me tell you, that sprightly grace and insinuating manner of yours will do some mischief among the
15 girls here.

Acres. Ah! you joke — ha! ha! mischief — ha! ha! but you know I am not my own property, my dear Lydia has forestalled me. She could never abide me in the country, because I used to dress so
20 badly — but odds frogs and tambours°! I shan't take matters so here, now ancient madam has no voice in it, I'll make my old clothes know who's master. I shall straightway cashier the hunting-frock, and render my leather breeches incapable.
25 My hair has been in training some time.

Abs. Indeed!

Acres. Ay — and thoff the side curls arc a little restive, my hind-part takes it very kindly.

Abs. Oh, you'll polish, I doubt not.

Acres. Absolutely I propose so — then if I can find out this Ensign Beverley, odds triggers and 5 flints! I'll make him know the difference o't.

Abs. Spoke like a man! But pray, Bob, I observe you have got an odd kind of a new method of swearing ——

Acres. Ha! ha! you've taken notice of it — 'tis 10 genteel, isn't it! — I didn't invent it myself though; but a commander in our militia, a great scholar, I assure you, says that there is no meaning in the common oaths, and that nothing but their antiquity makes them respectable; — because, he says, the 15 ancients would never stick to an oath or two, but would say, by Jove! or by Bacchus! or by Mars! or by Venus! or by Pallas, according to the sentiment: so that to swear with propriety, says my little major, the oath should be an echo to the sense; and this we 20 call the *oath referential* or *sentimental swearing* — ha! ha! 'tis genteel, isn't it?

Abs. Very genteel, and very new, indeed! — and I dare say will supplant all other figures of imprecation.

Acres. Ay, ay, the best terms will grow obsolete — 25 Damns have had their day.

Reënter FAG

Fag. Sir, there is a gentleman below desires to see you. — Shall I show him into the parlour?

Abs. Ay, you may.

Acres. Well, I must be gone ——

5 *Abs.* Stay; who is it, Fag?

Fag. Your father, sir.

Abs. You puppy, why didn't you show him up directly?   [*Exit* FAG.

Acres. You have business with Sir Anthony. —
10 I expect a message from Mrs. Malaprop at my lodgings. I have sent also to my dear friend Sir Lucius O'Trigger. Adieu, Jack! we must meet at night, when you shall give me a dozen bumpers to little Lydia.

15 *Abs.* That I will with all my heart. — [*Exit* ACRES.] Now for a parental lecture — I hope he has heard nothing of the business that has brought me here — I wish the gout had held him fast in Devonshire, with all my soul!

Enter SIR ANTHONY ABSOLUTE

20 Sir, I am delighted to see you here, looking so well! your sudden arrival at Bath made me apprehensive for your health.

Sir Anth. Very apprehensive, I dare say, Jack. —
What, you are recruiting here, hey?

Abs. Yes, sir, I am on duty.

Sir Anth. Well, Jack, I am glad to see you,
though I did not expect it, for I was going to write 5
to you on a little matter of business. — Jack, I
have been considering that I grow old and infirm,
and shall probably not trouble you long.

Abs. Pardon me, sir, I never saw you look more
strong and hearty; and I pray frequently that you 10
may continue so.

Sir Anth. I hope your prayers may be heard, with
all my heart. Well then, Jack, I have been considering that I am so strong and hearty I may
continue to plague you a long time. Now, Jack, I 15
am sensible that the income of your commission, and
what I have hitherto allowed you, is but a small
pittance for a lad of your spirit.

Abs. Sir, you are very good.

Sir Anth. And it is my wish, while yet I live, to 20
have my boy make some figure in the world. I have
resolved, therefore, to fix you at once in a noble independence.

Abs. Sir, your kindness overpowers me — such
generosity makes the gratitude of reason more lively 25
than the sensations even of filial affection.

Sir Anth. I am glad you are so sensible of my attention — and you shall be master of a large estate
in a few weeks.

    Abs. Let my future life, sir, speak my gratitude;
5 I cannot express the sense I have of your munifi-
cence. — Yet, sir, I presume you would not wish me
to quit the army?

    Sir Anth. Oh, that shall be as your wife chooses.

    Abs. My wife, sir!

10   *Sir Anth.* Ay, ay, settle that between you — settle
that between you.

    Abs. A wife, sir, did you say?

    Sir Anth. Ay, a wife — why, did not I mention
her before?

15   *Abs.* Not a word of her, sir.

    Sir Anth. Odd so! — I mustn't forget her though.
— Yes, Jack, the independence I was talking of is
by a marriage — the fortune is saddled with a wife —
but I suppose that makes no difference.

20   *Abs.* Sir! sir! — you amaze me!

    Sir Anth. Why, what's the matter with the fool?
Just now you were all gratitude and duty.

    Abs. I was, sir, — you talked to me of indepen-
dence and a fortune, but not a word of a wife.

25   *Sir Anth.* Why — what difference does that
make? Odds life, sir! if you have the estate,

you must take it with the live stock on it, as it
stands.

Abs. If my happiness is to be the price, I must
beg leave to decline the purchase. — Pray, sir, who
is the lady?   5

Sir Anth. What's that to you, sir? — Come, give
me your promise to love, and to marry her directly.

Abs. Surè, sir, this is not very reasonable, to
summon my affections for a lady I know nothing of!

Sir Anth. I am sure, sir, 'tis more unreasonable in 10
you to object to a lady you know nothing of.

Abs. Then, sir, I must tell you plainly that my
inclinations are fixed on another — my heart is engaged to an angel.

Sir Anth. Then pray let it send an excuse. It is 15
very sorry — but business prevents its waiting on
her.

Abs. But my vows are pledged to her.

Sir Anth. Let her foreclose, Jack; let her foreclose; they are not worth redeeming; besides, you 20
have the angel's vows in exchange, I suppose; so
there can be no loss there.

Abs. You must excuse me, sir, if I tell you, once
for all, that in this point I cannot obey you.

Sir Anth. Hark'ee, Jack; I have heard you for 25
some time with patience — I have been cool — quite

cool; but take care — you know I am compliance itself — when I am not thwarted; — no one more easily led — when I have my own way; — but don't put me in a frenzy.

5   *Abs.* Sir, I must repeat it — in this I cannot obey you.

Sir Anth. Now damn me! if ever I call you Jack again while I live!

Abs. Nay, sir, but hear me.

10   *Sir Anth.* Sir, I won't hear a word — not a word! not one word! so give me your promise by a nod — and I'll tell you what, Jack — I mean, you dog — if you don't, by ——

Abs. What, sir, promise to link myself to some
15 mass of ugliness! to ——

Sir Anth. Zounds! sirrah! the lady shall be as ugly as I choose: she shall have a lump on each shoulder; she shall be as crooked as the crescent; her one eye shall roll like the bull's in Cox's Museum°;
20 she shall have a skin like a mummy, and the beard of a Jew — she shall be all this, sirrah! — yet I will make you ogle her all day, and sit up all night to write sonnets on her beauty.

Abs. This is reason and moderation indeed!

25   *Sir Anth.* None of your sneering, puppy! no grinning, jackanapes!

Abs. Indeed, sir, I never was in a worse humour
for mirth in my life.

Sir Anth. 'Tis false, sir, I know you are laughing
in your sleeve; I know you'll grin when I am gone,
sirrah!   5

Abs. Sir, I hope I know my duty better.

Sir Anth. None of your passion, sir! none of your
violence, if you please! — It won't do with me, I
promise you.

Abs. Indeed, sir, I never was cooler in my life.   10

Sir Anth. 'Tis a confounded lie! — I know you
are in a passion in your heart; I know you are,
you hypocritical young dog! but it won't do.

Abs. Nay, sir, upon my word ——

Sir Anth. So you will fly out! can't you be cool 15
like me? What the devil good can passion do?
— Passion is of no service, you impudent, insolent,
overbearing reprobate! — There, you sneer again!
don't provoke me! — but you rely upon the mildness
of my temper — you do, you dog! you play upon the 20
meekness of my disposition! — Yet take care — the
patience of a saint may be overcome at last! — but
mark! I give you six hours and a half to consider
of this: if you then agree, without any condition, to
do everything on earth that I choose, why — con- 25
found you! I may in time forgive you. — If not,

zounds! don't enter the same hemisphere with me!
don't dare to breathe the same air, or use the same
light with me; but get an atmosphere and a sun of
your own! I'll strip you of your commission; I'll
5 lodge a five-and-threepence in the hands of trustees,
and you shall live on the interest. — I'll disown you,
I'll disinherit you, I'll unget you! and damn me!
if ever I call you Jack again!   [Exit.

    Abs. Mild, gentle, considerate father — I kiss your
10 hands!   What a tender method of giving his opinion
· in these matters Sir Anthony has! I dare not trust
him with the truth. — I wonder what old wealthy
hag it is that he wants to bestow on me! — Yet he
married himself for love! and was in his youth a bold
15 intriguer, and a gay companion!

Reënter FAG.

    Fag. Assuredly, sir, your father is wrath to a
degree; he comes down stairs eight or ten steps at
a time — muttering, growling, and thumping the
banisters all the way: I and the cook's dog stand
20 bowing at the door — rap! he gives me a stroke
on the head with his cane; bids me carry that to my
master; then kicking the poor turnspit° into the area,
damns us all, for a puppy triumvirate! — Upon my

credit, sir, were I in your place, and found my father such very bad company, I should certainly drop his acquaintance.

Abs. Cease your impertinence, sir, at present. — Did you come in for nothing more? — Stand out of 5 the way!   [*Pushes him aside and exit.*

Fag. So! Sir Anthony trims my master: he is afraid to reply to his father — then vents his spleen on poor Fag! When one is vexed by one person, to revenge one's self on another, who happens to come 10 in the way, is the vilest injustice! Ah! it shows the worst temper — the basest ——

Enter BOY

Boy. Mr. Fag; Mr. Fag! your master calls you.

Fag. Well, you little dirty puppy, you need not bawl so! — The meanest disposition! the ——   15

Boy. Quick, quick, Mr. Fag!

Fag. Quick! quick! you impudent jackanapes! am I to be commanded by you too? you little impertinent, insolent, kitchen-bred ——

[*Exit kicking and beating him.*

E

SCENE II.   *The North Parade*

Enter LUCY

Lucy. So — I shall have another rival to add to
my mistress' list — Captain Absolute.   However,
I shall not enter his name till my purse has received
notice in form.   Poor Acres is dismissed! — Well,
5 I have done him a last friendly office, in letting him
know that Beverley was here before him. — Sir
Lucius is generally more punctual, when he expects
to hear from his *dear Dalia*, as he calls her: I wonder
he's not here! — I have a little scruple of conscience
10 from this deceit; though I should not be paid so well,
if my hero knew that Delia was near fifty, and her
own mistress.

Enter SIR LUCIUS O'TRIGGER

Sir Luc. Ha! my little ambassadress — upon my
conscience, I have been looking for you; I have been
15 on the South Parade° this half hour.
Lucy. [*Speaking simply.*]   O gemini! and I have
been waiting for your worship here on the North.
Sir Luc. Faith! — may be that was the reason we
did not meet; and it is very comical too, how you

could go out and I not see you — for I was only
taking a nap at the Parade Coffee-house, and I
chose the window on purpose that I might not miss
you.

Lucy. My stars! Now I'd wager a sixpence I 5
went by while you were asleep.

Sir Luc. Sure enough it must have been so — and
I never dreamt it was so late, till I waked. Well,
but my little girl, have you got nothing for me?

Lucy. Yes, but I have — I've got a letter for you 10
in my pocket.

Sir Luc. O faith! I guessed you weren't come
empty-handed. — Well — let me see what the dear
creature says.

Lucy. There, Sir Lucius.   [*Gives him a letter.* 15

Sir Luc. [Reads.] *Sir — there is often a sudden
incentive impulse in love, that has a greater induction
than years of domestic combination: such. was the
commotion I felt at the first superfluous view of Sir
Lucius O'Trigger.* — Very pretty, upon my word. — 20
*Female punctuation forbids me to say more, yet let me
add, that it will give me joy infallible to find Sir Lucius
worthy the last criterion of my affections.*   DELIA.
Upon my conscience! Lucy, your lady is a great
mistress of language. Faith, she's quite the queen 25
of the dictionary! — for the devil a word dare refuse

coming at her call — though one would think it was
quite out of hearing.

Lucy. Ay, sir, a lady of her experience ——

Sir Luc. Experience! what, at seventeen?

5   *Lucy.* O true, sir — but then she reads so — my
stars! how she will read off hand!

Sir Luc. Faith, she must be very deep read to
write this way — though she is rather an arbitrary
writer too — for here are a great many poor words
10 pressed into the service of this note, that would get
their *habeas corpus* from any court in Christendom.

Lucy. Ah! Sir Lucius, if you were to hear how
she talks of you!

Sir Luc. Oh, tell her I'll make her the best husband
15 in the world, and Lady O'Trigger into the bargain.
—But we must get the old gentlewoman's consent —
and do everything fairly.

Lucy. Nay, Sir Lucius, I thought you wa'n't rich
enough to be so nice!

20   *Sir Luc.* Upon my word, young woman, you
have hit it: — I am so poor, that I can't afford to
do a dirty action. — If I did not want money, I'd
steal your mistress and her fortune with a great deal
of pleasure. — However, my pretty girl, [*Gives her
25 money,*] here's a little something to buy you a ribbon;
and meet me in the evening, and I'll give you an

answer to this.　So, hussy, take a kiss beforehand to
put you in mind.　　　　　　　　　　　*[Kisses her.*

Lucy.　O Lud! Sir Lucius — I never seed such a
gemman! My lady won't like you if you're so
impudent.　　　　　　　　　　　　　　　　5

Sir Luc.　Faith she will, Lucy! — That same —
pho! what's the name of it? — modesty — is a
quality in a lover more praised by the women than
liked; so, if your mistress asks you whether Sir
Lucius ever gave you a kiss, tell her fifty — my dear. 10

Lucy.　What, would you have me tell her a lie?

Sir Luc.　Ah, then, you baggage! I'll make it a
truth presently.

Lucy.　For shame now! here is some one coming.

Sir Luc.　Oh, faith, I'll quiet your conscience!　15
　　　　　　　　　　　[Exit, humming a tune.
　　　　　　　　　Enter FAG

Fag.　So, so, ma'am! I humbly beg pardon.

Lucy.　O Lud! now, Mr. Fag — you flurry one
so.

Fag.　Come, come, Lucy, here's no one by — so a
little less simplicity, with a grain or two more sin- 20
cerity, if you please. — You play false with us,
madam — I saw you give the baronet a letter. My
master shall know this — and if he don't call him out,
I will.

Lucy. Ha! ha! ha! you gentlemen's gentlemen are so hasty. — That letter was from Mrs. Malaprop, simpleton. — She is taken with Sir Lucius's address.

Fag. How! what tastes some people have! —
5 Why, I suppose I have walked by her window a hundred times. — But what says our young lady? any message to my master?

Lucy. Sad news, Mr. Fag. — A worse rival than Acres! Sir Anthony Absolute has proposed his son.
10 *Fag.* What, Captain Absolute?

Lucy. Even so — I overheard it all.

Fag. Ha! ha! ha! very good, faith. Good bye, Lucy, I must away with this news.

Lucy. Well, you may laugh — but it is true, I
15 assure you. — [*Going.*] But, Mr. Fag, tell your master not to be cast down by this.

Fag. Oh, he'll be so disconsolate!

Lucy. And charge him not to think of quarelling with young Absolute.
20 *Fag.* Never fear! never fear!

Lucy. Be sure—bid him keep up his spirits.

Fag. We will—we will.   [*Exeunt severally.*

ACT III

Scene I. *The North Parade*

Enter Captain Absolute

Abs. 'Tis just as Fag told me, indeed. Whimsical enough, faith! My father wants to force me to marry the very girl I am plotting to run away with! He must not know of my connection with her yet awhile. He has too summary a method of proceeding 5 in these matters. However, I'll read my recantation instantly. My conversion is something sudden, indeed — but I can assure him it is very sincere. So, so — here he comes. He looks plaguy gruff.

[*Steps aside.*

Enter Sir Anthony Absolute

Sir Anth. No. — I'll die sooner than forgive him. 10 Die, did I say? I'll live these fifty years to plague him. At our last meeting, his impudence had almost put me out of temper. An obstinate, passionate, self-willed boy! Who can he take after? This is my return for getting him before all his brothers 15 and sisters! — for putting him, at twelve years old, into a marching regiment, and allowing him fifty

55

pounds a year, besides his pay, ever since! But I
have done with him; he's anybody's son for me.
I never will see him more, never — never — never.

Abs. [*Aside, coming forward.*] Now for a peni-
5 tential face.

Sir Anth. Fellow, get out of my way!

Abs. Sir, you see a penitent before you.

Sir Anth. I see an impudent scoundrel before me.

Abs. A sincere penitent. I am come, sir, to ac-
10 knowledge my error, and to submit entirely to your
will.

Sir Anth. What's that?

Abs. I have been revolving, and reflecting, and
considering on your past goodness, and kindness,
15 and condescension to me.

Sir Anth. Well, sir?

Abs. I have been likewise weighing and balancing
what you were pleased to mention concerning duty,
and obedience, and authority.

20 *Sir Anth.* Well, puppy?

Abs. Why then, sir, the result of my reflections is
— a resolution to sacrifice every inclination of my
own to your satisfaction.

Sir Anth. Why now you talk sense — absolute
25 sense — I never heard anything more sensible in
my life. Confound you! you shall be Jack again.

Abs. I am happy in the appellation.

Sir Anth. Why then, Jack, my dear Jack, I will now inform you who the lady really is. Nothing but your passion and violence, you silly fellow, prevented my telling you at first. Prepare, Jack, for 5 wonder and rapture — prepare. What think you of Miss Lydia Languish?

Abs. Languish! What, the Languishes of Worcestershire?

Sir Anth. Worcestershire! no. Did you never 10 meet Mrs. Malaprop and her niece, Miss Languish, who came into our country just before you were last ordered to your regiment!

Abs. Malaprop! Languish! I don't remember ever to have heard the names before. Yet, stay — 15 I think I do recollect something. Languish! Languish! She squints, don't she? A little red-haired girl?

Sir Anth. Squints! A red-haired girl! Zounds! no. 20

Abs. Then I must have forgot; it can't be the same person.

Sir Anth. Jack! Jack! what think you of blooming, love-breathing seventeen?

Abs. As to that, sir, I am quite indifferent. If I 25 can please you in the matter, 'tis all I desire.

Sir Anth. Nay, but Jack, such eyes! such eyes!
so innocently wild! so bashfully irresolute! not a
glance but speaks and kindles some thought of love!
Then, Jack, her cheeks! her cheeks, Jack! so deeply
5 blushing at the insinuations of her tell-tale eyes!
Then, Jack, her lips! O Jack, lips smiling at their
own discretion; and if not smiling, more sweetly
pouting; more lovely in sullenness!

Abs. That's she indeed. Well done, old gentle-
10 man.   [*Aside.*

Sir Anth. Then, Jack, her neck! O Jack!
Jack!

Abs. And which is to be mine, sir, the niece, or
the aunt?

15 *Sir Anth.* Why, you unfeeling, insensible puppy,
I despise you! When I was of your age, such a
description would have made me fly like a rocket!
The aunt indeed! Odds life! when I ran away with
your mother, I would not have touched anything
20 old or ugly to gain an empire.

Abs. Not to please your father, sir?

Sir Anth. To please my father! zounds! not to
please — Oh, my father — odd so! — yes — yes;
if my father indeed had desired — that's quite an-
25 other matter. Though he wa'n't the indulgent
father that I am, Jack.

Abs. I dare say not, sir.

Sir Anth. But, Jack, you are not sorry to find your mistress is so beautiful?

Abs. Sir, I repeat it — if I please you in this affair, 'tis all I desire.   Not that I think a woman the 5 worse for being handsome; but, sir, if you please to recollect, you before hinted something about a hump or two, one eye, and a few more graces of that kind — now, without being very nice, I own I should rather choose a wife of mine to have the usual number of 10 limbs, and a limited quantity of back: and though one eye may be very agreeable, yet as the prejudice has always run in favour of two, I would not wish to affect a singularity in that article.

Sir Anth. What a phlegmatic sot it is!   Why, 15 sirrah, you're an anchorite! — a vile, insensible stock.   You a soldier! — you're a walking block, fit only to dust the company's regimentals on!   Odds life!   I have a great mind to marry the girl myself.

Abs. I am entirely at your disposal, sir: if you 20 should think of addressing Miss Languish yourself, I suppose you would have me marry the aunt; or if you should change your mind, and take the old lady — 'tis the same to me — I'll marry the niece.   25

Sir Anth. Upon my word, Jack, thou'rt either a

very great hypocrite, or — but, come, I know your
indifference on such a subject must be all a lie —
I'm sure it must — come, now — come, confess Jack
— you have been lying — ha'n't you? You have
5 been playing the hypocrite, hey! — I'll never forgive you, if you ha'n't been lying and playing the
hypocrite.

Abs. I'm sorry, sir, that the respect and duty
which I bear to you should be so mistaken.

10 *Sir Anth.* Hang your respect and duty! But
come along with me, I'll write a note to Mrs. Malaprop, and you shall visit the lady directly. Her
eyes shall be the Promethean torch to you — come
along, I'll never forgive you, if you don't come back
15 stark mad with rapture and impatience — if you
don't, egad, I will marry the girl myself! [*Exeunt.*

SCENE II. *Julia's Dressing-room*

FAULKLAND *discovered alone*

Faulk. They told me Julia would return directly;
I wonder she is not yet come! How mean does this
captious, unsatisfied temper of mine appear to my
20 cooler judgment! Yet I know not that I indulge it
in any other point: but on this one subject, and to

this one subject, whom I think I love beyond my life,
I am ever ungenerously fretful and madly capricious!
I am conscious of it — yet I cannot correct myself!
What tender honest joy sparkled in her eyes when
we met! how delicate was the warmth of her ex- 5
pressions! I was ashamed to appear less happy —
though I had come resolved to wear a face of coolness
and upbraiding. Sir Anthony's presence prevented
my proposed expostulations: Yet I must be satisfied
that she has not been so very happy in my absence. 10
She is coming! Yes! — I know the nimbleness of
her tread, when she thinks her impatient Faulkland
counts the moments of her stay.

Enter JULIA

Jul. I had not hoped to see you again so soon.
Faulk. Could I, Julia, be contented with my first 15
welcome — restrained as we were by the presence of
a third person?
Jul. O Faulkland, when your kindness can make
me thus happy, let me not think that I discovered
something of coldness in your first salutation. 20
Faulk. 'Twas but your fancy, Julia. I was
rejoiced to see you — to see you in such health.
Sure I had no cause for coldness?

Jul. Nay then, I see you have taken something
ill. You must not conceal from me what it is.

Faulk. Well, then — shall I own to you that my
joy at hearing of your health and arrival here, by
5 your neighbour Acres, was somewhat damped by
his dwelling much on the high spirits you had enjoyed in Devonshire — on your mirth — your singing — dancing — and I know not what! For such
is my temper, Julia, that I should regard every
10 mirthful moment in your absence as a treason to
constancy. The mutual tear that steals down the
cheek of parting lovers is a compact, that no smile
shall live there till they meet again.

Jul. Must I never cease to tax my Faulkland with
15 this teasing minute caprice? Can the idle reports
of a silly boor weigh in your breast against my
tried affection?

Faulk. They have no weight with me, Julia:
No, no — I am happy if you have been so — yet
20 only say, that you did not sing with mirth — say
that you thought of Faulkland in the dance.

Jul. I never can be happy in your absence. If I
wear a countenance of content, it is to show that my
mind holds no doubt of my Faulkland's truth. If I
25 seemed sad, it were to make malice triumph; and
say, that I had fixed my heart on one, who left me

to lament his roving, and my own credulity. Believe
me, Faulkland, I mean not to upbraid you, when
I say, that I have often dressed sorrow in smiles,
lest my friends should guess whose unkindness had
caused my tears.   5

Faulk. You were ever all goodness to me. Oh, I
am a brute, when I but admit a doubt of your true
constancy !

Jul. If ever without such cause from you, as I will
not suppose possible, you find my affections veer- 10
ing but a point, may I become a proverbial scoff for
levity and base ingratitude.

Faulk. Ah ! Julia, that last word is grating to me.
I would I had no title to your gratitude ! Search
your heart, Julia; perhaps what you have mistaken 15
for love, is but the warm effusion of a too thankful
heart.

Jul. For what quality must I love you?

Faulk. For no quality ! To regard me for any
quality of mind or understanding, were only to 20
esteem me. And for person — I have often wished
myself deformed, to be convinced that I owed no
obligation there for any part of your affection.

Jul. Where nature has bestowed a show of nice
attention in the features of a man, he should laugh 25
at it as misplaced. I have seen men, who in this

vain article, perhaps, might rank above you; but
my heart has never asked my eyes if it were so or not.

Faulk. Now this is not well from you, Julia — I
despise person in a man — yet if you loved me as I
5 wish, though I were an Æthiop, you'd think none so
fair.

Jul. I see you are determined to be unkind!
The contract which my poor father bound us in
gives you more than a lover's privilege.

10 *Faulk.* Again, Julia, you raise ideas that feed and
justify my doubts. I would not have been more
free — no — I am proud of my restraint. Yet —
yet — perhaps your high respect alone for this
solemn compact has fettered your inclinations, which
15 else had made a worthier choice. How shall I be
sure, had you remained unbound in thought and
promise, that I should still have been the object of
your persevering love?

Jul. Then try me now. Let us be free as strangers
20 as to what is past: my heart will not feel more
liberty!

Faulk. There now! so hasty, Julia! so anxious to
be free! If your love for me were fixed and ardent, you
would not lose your hold, even though I wished it!

25 *Jul.* Oh! you torture me to the heart! I cannot
bear it.

Faulk. I do not mean to distress you. If I loved you less I should never give you an uneasy moment. But hear me. All my fretful doubts arise from this. Women are not used to weigh and separate the motives of their affections: the cold dictates of 5 prudence, gratitude, or filial duty, may sometimes be mistaken for the pleadings of the heart. I would not boast — yet let me say, that I have neither age, person, nor character, to found dislike on; my fortune such as few ladies could be charged with indis- 10 cretion in the match. O Julia! when love receives such countenance from prudence, nice minds will be suspicious of its birth.

Jul. I know not whither your insinuations would tend: — but as they seem pressing to insult me, 15 I will spare you the regret of having done so. — I have given you no cause for this! [*Exit in tears.*

Faulk. In tears! Stay, Julia: stay but for a moment. — The door is fastened! — Julia! — my soul — but for one moment! — I hear her sobbing! — 20 'Sdeath! what a brute am I to use her thus! Yet stay. — Ay — she is coming now: — how little resolution there is in woman! — how a few soft words can turn them! — No, faith! — she is not coming either. — Why, Julia — my love — say but 25 that you forgive me — come but to tell me that —

F

now this is being too resentful.   Stay ! she is coming
too — I thought she would — no steadiness in any
thing : her going away must have been a mere trick
then — she *sha'n't* see that I was hurt by it. — I'll
5 affect indifference — [*Hums a tune: then listens.*]
No — zounds ! she's not coming ! — nor don't intend it, I suppose. — This is not steadiness, but
obstinacy !   Yet I deserve it. — What, after so long
an absence to quarrel with her tenderness ! — 'twas
10 barbarous and unmanly ! — I should be ashamed
to see her now. — I'll wait till her just resentment is
abated — and when I distress her so again, may I
lose her forever, and be linked instead to some antique
virago, whose gnawing passions, and long hoarded
15 spleen, shall make me curse my folly half the day
and all the night !   [*Exit.*

SCENE III.   *Mrs. Malaprop's Lodgings*
MRS. MALAPROP, *with a letter in her hand,*
and CAPTAIN ABSOLUTE

Mrs. Mal. Your being Sir Anthony's son, captain, would itself be a sufficient accommodation°;
but from the ingenuity° of your appearance, I am
20 convinced you deserve the character here given of
you.

Abs. Permit me to say, madam, that as I never yet have had the pleasure of seeing Miss Languish, my principal inducement in this affair at present is the honour of being allied to Mrs. Malaprop; of whose intellectual accomplishments, elegant manners, 5 and unaffected learning, no tongue is silent.

Mrs. Mal. Sir, you do me infinite honour! I beg, captain, you'll be seated. — [*They sit.*] Ah! few gentlemen, now-a-days, know how to value the ineffectual° qualities in a woman! few think how a 10 little knowledge becomes a gentlewoman! — Men have no sense now but for the worthless flower of beauty!

Abs. It is but too true, indeed, ma'am; — yet I fear our ladies should share the blame — they think 15 our admiration of beauty so great, that knowledge in them would be superfluous. Thus, like garden-trees, they seldom show fruit, till time has robbed them of the more specious blossom. — Few, like Mrs. Malaprop and the orange-tree, are rich in both 20 at once.

Mrs. Mal. Sir, you overpower me with good-breeding. — He is the very pine-apple° of polite-ness! — You are not ignorant, captain, that this giddy girl has somehow contrived to fix her affections 25 on a beggarly, strolling, eaves-dropping ensign,

whom none of us have seen, and nobody knows
anything of.

 Abs. Oh, I have heard the silly affair before. —
I'm not at all prejudiced against her on that account.

5 *Mrs. Mal.* You are very good and very consider-
ate, captain. I am sure I have done everything in
my power since I exploded° the affair; long ago I
laid my positive conjunctions° on her, never to think
on the fellow again; — I have since laid Sir Anthony's

10 preposition° before her; but, I am sorry to say, she
seems resolved to decline every particle° that I enjoin her.

 Abs. It must be very distressing, indeed, ma'am.

 Mrs. Mal. Oh! it gives me the hydrostatics°

15 to such a degree! — I thought she had persisted°
from corresponding with him; but, behold, this very
day, I have interceded° another letter from the fellow;
I believe I have it in my pocket.

 Abs. Oh, the devil! my last note. · [*Aside.*

20 *Mrs. Mal.* Ay, here it is.

 Abs. Ay, my note indeed! O the little traitress
Lucy. ·   [*Aside.*

 Mrs. Mal. There, perhaps you may know the
writing.   [*Gives him the letter.*

25 *Abs.* I think I have seen the hand before — yes, I
certainly must have seen this hand before —

Mrs. Mal. Nay, but read it, captain.

Abs. [Reads.] *My soul's idol, my adored Lydia!*
— Very tender indeed!

Mrs. Mal. Tender! ay, and profane too, o' my
conscience.   5

Abs. [Reads.] *I am excessively alarmed at the
intelligence you send me, the more so as my new
rival* ——

Mrs. Mal. That's you, sir.

Abs. [Reads.] *Has universally the character of* 10
*being an accomplished gentleman and a man of
honour.*   Well, that's handsome enough.

Mrs. Mal. Oh, the fellow has some design in
writing so.

Abs. That he had, I'll answer for him, ma'am.   15

Mrs. Mal. But go on, sir — you'll see presently.

Abs. [Reads.] *As for the old weather-beaten she-
dragon who guards you* — Who can he mean by that?

Mrs. Mal. Me, sir! — me! — he means me! —
There — what do you think now? — but go on a 20
little further.

Abs. Impudent scoundrel! — [Reads.] *it shall go
hard but I will elude her vigilance, as I am told that the
same ridiculous vanity, which makes her dress up her
coarse features, and deck her dull chat with hard words* 25
which she don't understand ——

Mrs. Mal. There, sir, an attack upon my language! what do you think of that? — an aspersion upon my parts of speech! was ever such a brute! Sure, if I reprehend° any thing in this world, it is the use of 5 my oracular° tongue, and a nice derangement° of epitaphs°!

Abs. He deserves to be hanged and quartered! let me see — [Reads.] *same ridiculous vanity* ——

Mrs. Mal. You need not read it again, sir.

10 *Abs.* I beg pardon, ma'am. — [Reads.] *does also lay her open to the grossest deceptions from flattery and pretended admiration* — an impudent coxcomb! — *so that I have a scheme to see you shortly with the old harridan's consent, and even to make her* 15 *a go-between in our interview.* — Was ever such assurance!

Mrs. Mal. Did you ever hear anything like it? — he'll elude my vigilance, will he — yes, yes! ha! ha! he's very likely to enter these doors; we'll try 20 who can plot best!

Abs. So we will, ma'am — so we will! Ha! ha! ha! a conceited puppy, ha! ha! ha! — Well, but, Mrs. Malaprop, as the girl seems so infatuated by this fellow, suppose you were to wink at her correspond-25 ing with him for a little time — let her even plot an elopement with him — then do you connive at her

escape — while I, just in the nick, will have the
fellow laid by the heels, and fairly contrive to carry
her off in his stead.

Mrs. Mal. I am delighted with the scheme; never
was anything better perpetrated!   5

Abs. But, pray, could not I see the lady for a few
minutes now? — I should like to try her temper a
little.

Mrs. Mal. Why, I don't know — I doubt she is
not prepared for a visit of this kind.   There is a 10
decorum in these matters.

Abs. O Lord! she won't mind me — only tell her
Beverley ——

Mrs. Mal. Sir!

Abs. Gently, good tongue.   [*Aside.* 15

Mrs. Mal. What did you say of Beverley?

Abs. Oh, I was going to propose that you should .
tell her, by way of jest, that it was Beverley who was
below; she'd come down fast enough then — ha!
ha! ha!   20

Mrs. Mal. 'Twould be a trick she well deserves;
besides, you know the fellow tells her he'll get my
consent to see her — ha! ha!   Let him if he can, I
say again.   Lydia, come down here! — [*Calling.*]
He'll make me a go-between in their interviews! — 25
ha! ha! ha! Come down, I say, Lydia! I don't

wonder at your laughing, ha! ha! ha! his impudence is truly ridiculous.

Abs. 'Tis very ridiculous, upon my soul, ma'am,
ha! ha! ha!

5 *Mrs. Mal.* The little hussy won't hear. Well,
I'll go and tell her at once who it is — she shall
know that Captain Absolute is come to wait on her.
And I'll make her behave as becomes a young woman.

Abs. As you please, ma'am.

10 *Mrs. Mal.* For the present, captain, your servant.
Ah! you've not done laughing yet, I see — elude
my vigilance; yes, yes; ha! ha! ha!   [*Exit.*

Abs. Ha! ha! ha! one would think now that I
might throw off all disguise at once, and seize my
15 prize with security; but such is Lydia's caprice,
that to undeceive were probably to lose her. I'll
see whether she knows me.

[*Walks aside, and seems engaged in looking at the
pictures.*

Enter LYDIA

Lyd. What a scene am I now to go through!
surely nothing can be more dreadful than to be
20 obliged to listen to the loathsome addresses of a
stranger to one's heart. I have heard of girls per-

seocuted as I am, who have appealed in behalf of their
favoured lover to the generosity of his rival; suppose I were to try it — there stands the hated rival —
an officer too! — but oh, how unlike my Beverley!
I wonder he don't begin — truly he seems a very 5
negligent wooer! — quite at his ease, upon my word!
— I'll speak first — Mr. Absolute.

Abs. Ma'am.   [*Turns round.*

Lyd. O heavens! Beverley!

Abs. Hush! — hush, my life! softly! be not 10
surprised!

Lyd. I am so astonished! and so terrified! and
so overjoyed! — for Heaven's sake! how came you
here?

Abs. Briefly, I have deceived your aunt — I was 15
informed that my new rival was to visit here this
evening, and contriving to have him kept away, have
passed myself on her for Captain Absolute.

Lyd. O charming! And she really takes you
for young Absolute!   20

Abs. Oh, she's convinced of it.

Lyd. Ha! ha! ha! I can't forbear laughing to
think how her sagacity is overreached!

Abs. But we trifle with our precious moments
— such another opportunity may not occur; then 25
let me now conjure my kind, my condescending

angel, to fix the time when I may rescue her from
undeserving persecution, and with a licensed warmth
plead for my reward.

    Lyd. Will you then, Beverley, consent to forfeit
5 that portion of my paltry wealth? — that burden
on the wings of love?

    Abs. Oh, come to me — rich only thus — in
loveliness! Bring no portion to me but thy love
— 'twill be generous in you, Lydia — for well
10 you know, it is the only dower your poor Beverley
can repay.

    Lyd. How persuasive are his words! — how
charming will poverty be with him!   [*Aside.*

    Abs. Ah! my soul, what a life will we then live!
15 Love shall be our idol and support! we will worship him with a monastic strictness; abjuring all
worldly toys, to centre every thought and action
there. Proud of calamity, we will enjoy the wreck
of wealth; while the surrounding gloom of adver-
20 sity shall make the flame of our pure love show
doubly bright. By Heavens! I would fling all
goods of fortune from me with a prodigal hand,
to enjoy the scene where I might clasp my Lydia
to my bosom, and say, the world affords no smile
25 to me but here — [*Embracing her.*] If she holds
out now, the devil is in it!   [*Aside.*

Lyd. Now could I fly with him to the antipodes!
but my persecution is not yet come to a crisis.
                                                [*Aside.*

Reënter Mrs. Malaprop, *listening*

Mrs. Mal. I am impatient to know how the little
hussy deports herself.   [*Aside.*
Abs. So pensive, Lydia! — is then your warmth 5
abated?
Mrs. Mal. Warmth abated! — so! — she has
been in a passion, I suppose.   .   [*Aside.*
Lyd. No — nor ever can while I have life.
Mrs. Mal. An ill-tempered little devil! She'll be 10
in a passion all her life — will she?   [*Aside.*
Lyd. Think not the idle threats of my ridiculous
aunt can ever have any weight with me.
Mrs. Mal. Very dutiful, upon my word! [*Aside.*
Lyd. Let her choice be Captain Absolute, but 15
Beverley is mine.
Mrs. Mal. I am astonished at her assurance! —
to his face — this is to his face!   [*Aside.*
Abs. Thus then let me enforce my suit.
                                             [*Kneeling.*
Mrs. Mal. [*Aside.*] Ay, poor young man! — 20
down on his knees entreating for pity! — I can

contain no longer. — [*Coming forward.*] Why, thou
vixen! — I have overheard you.

    Abs. Oh, confound her vigilance!   [*Aside.*

    Mrs. Mal. Captain Absolute, I know not how to
5 apologize for her shocking rudeness.

    Abs. [*Aside.*] So all's safe, I find. — [*Aloud.*]
I have hopes, madam, that time will bring the
young lady ——

    Mrs. Mal. Oh, there's nothing to be hoped for
10 from her! she's as headstrong as an allegory° on
the banks of Nile.

    Lyd. Nay, madam, what do you charge me with
now?

    Mrs. Mal. Why, thou unblushing rebel — didn't
15 you tell this gentleman to his face that you loved
another better? — didn't you say you never would
be his?

    Lyd. No, madam — I did not.

    Mrs. Mal. Good Heavens! what assurance! —
20 Lydia, Lydia, you ought to know that lying don't
become a young woman! — Didn't you boast that
Beverley, that stroller Beverley, possessed your
heart? — Tell me that, I say.

    Lyd. 'Tis true, ma'am, and none but Beverley ——
25   *Mrs. Mal.* Hold! — hold, Assurance! — you shall
not be so rude.

Abs. Nay, pray, Mrs. Malaprop, don't stop the young lady's speech: she's very welcome to talk thus — it does not hurt me in the least, I assure you.

Mrs. Mal. You are too good, captain — too 5 amiably patient — but come with me, miss. — Let us see you again soon, captain — remember what we have fixed.

Abs. I shall, ma'am.

Mrs. Mal. Come, take a graceful leave of the 10 gentleman.

Lyd. May every blessing wait on my Beverley, my loved Bev——

Mrs. Mal. Hussy! I'll choke the word in your throat! — come along — come along. 15

[*Exeunt severally;* CAPTAIN ABSOLUTE *kissing his hand to* LYDIA — MRS. MALAPROP *stopping her from speaking.*

SCENE IV. *Acres' Lodgings*

ACRES, *as just dressed, and* DAVID

Acres. Indeed, David — do you think I become it so?

Dav. You are quite another creature, believe

me, master, by the mass! an we've any luck we
shall see the Devon monkerony° in all the print-
shops in Bath°!

    Acres. Dress does make a difference, David.

5   *Dav.* 'Tis all in all, I think. — Difference! why,
an you were to go now to Clod-hall, I am certain
the old lady wouldn't know you: master Butler
wouldn't believe his own eyes, and Mrs. Pickle
would cry, Lard presarve me! Our dairy-maid
10 would come giggling to the door, and I warrant
Dolly Tester, your honour's favourite, would blush
like my waistcoat. — Oons! I'll hold a gallon,
there an't a dog in the house but would bark, and
I question whether Phillis would wag a hair of her
15 tail!

    Acres. Ay, David, there's nothing like polishing.

    Dav. So I says of your honour's boots; but the
boy never heeds me!

    Acres. But, David, has Mr. De-la-grace been
20 here? I must rub up my balancing, and chasing,
and boring.°

    Dav. I'll call again, sir.

    Acres. Do — and see if there are any letters for
me at the post-office.

25   *Dav.* I will. — By the mass, I can't help looking
at your head! — if I hadn't been at the cooking,

I wish I may die if I should have known the dish
again myself!   [*Exit.*
  Acres. [*Practising a dancing-step.*] Sink, slide —
coupee.° — Confound the first inventors of cotillons! say I — they are as bad as algebra to us 5
country gentlemen — I can walk a minuet easy
enough when I am forced! — and I have been accounted a good stick in a country-dance. — Odds
jigs and tabors! I never valued your cross-over to
couple — figure in — right and left — and I'd foot 10
it with e'er a captain in the county! — but these
outlandish heathen allemandes° and cotillons are
quite beyond me! — I shall never prosper at 'em,
that's sure — mine are true-born English legs —
they don't understand their curst French lingo! — 15
their *pas* this, and *pas* that, and *pas* t'other! —
my feet don't like to be called paws! no, 'tis certain
I have most Antigallican° toes!

Enter SERVANT

  Serv. Here is Sir Lucius O'Trigger to wait on
you, sir.   20
  Acres. Show him in.
                              [*Exit* SERVANT.

Enter SIR LUCIUS O'TRIGGER

Sir Luc. Mr. Acres, I am delighted to embrace you.

Acres. My dear Sir Lucius, I kiss your hands.

Sir Luc. Pray, my friend, what has brought you 5 so suddenly to Bath?

Acres. Faith! I have followed Cupid's Jack-a-lantern,° and find myself in a quagmire at last. — In short, I have been very ill-used, Sir Lucius.— I don't choose to mention names, but look on me 10 as on a very ill-used gentleman.

Sir Luc. Pray what is the case? — I ask no names.

Acres. Mark me, Sir Lucius, I fall as deep as need be in love with a young lady — her friends take 15 my part — I follow her to Bath — send word of my arrival; and receive answer, that the lady is to be otherwise disposed of. — This, Sir Lucius, I call being ill-used.

Sir Luc. Very ill, upon my conscience. — Pray, 20 can you divine the cause of it?

Acres. Why, there's the matter; she has another lover, one Beverley, who, I am told, is now in Bath. — Odds slanders and lies! he must be at the bottom of it.

Sir Luc. A rival in the case, is there? — and you think he has supplanted you unfairly?

Acres. Unfairly! to be sure he has. He never could have done it fairly.

Sir Luc. Then sure you know what is to be 5 done!

Acres. Not I, upon my soul!

Sir Luc. We wear no swords here, but you understand me.

Acres. What! fight him!   . 10

Sir Luc. Ay, to be sure: what can I mean else?

Acres. But he has given me no provocation.

Sir Luc. Now, I think he has given you the greatest provocation in the world. Can a man commit a more heinous offence against another 15 than to fall in love with the same woman? Oh, by my soul! it is the most unpardonable breach of friendship.

Acres. Breach of friendship! ay, ay; but I have no acquaintance with this man. I never saw him 20 in my life.

Sir Luc. That's no argument at all — he has the less right then to take such a liberty.

Acres. Gad, that's true — I grow full of anger, Sir Lucius! — I fire apace! Odds hilts and blades! 25 I find a man may have a deal of valour in him, and

G

not know it! But couldn't I contrive to have a
little right of my side?

Sir Luc. What the devil signifies right, when
your honour is concerned? Do you think Achilles,
5 or my little Alexander the Great, ever inquired
where the right lay? No, by my soul, they drew
their broadswords, and left the lazy sons of peace
to settle the justice of it.

Acres. Your words are a grenadier's march to
10 my heart! I believe courage must be catching!
I certainly do feel a kind of valour rising as it were
— a kind of courage, as I may say. — Odds flints,
pans, and triggers! I'll challenge him directly.

Sir Luc. Ah, my little friend, if I had Blunder-
15 buss Hall here, I could show you a range of ances-
try, in the O'Trigger line, that would furnish the
new room; every one of whom had killed his
man! — For though the mansion-house and dirty
acres have slipped through my fingers, I thank
20 heaven our honour and the family-pictures are as
fresh as ever.

Acres. O, Sir Lucius! I have had ancestors too!
— every man of 'em colonel or captain in the
militia! — Odds balls and barrels! say no more
25 — I'm braced for it. The thunder of your words
has soured the milk of human kindness in my

breast; — Zounds! as the man in the play says,
I could do such deeds°!

  Sir Luc. Come, come, there must be no passion
at all in the case — these things should always be
done civilly.   5

  Acres. I must be in a passion, Sir Lucius —
I must be in a rage. — Dear Sir Lucius, let me be
in a rage, if you love me. Come, here's pen and
paper. — [*Sits down to write.*] I would the ink
were red! — Indite, I say indite! — How shall 10
I begin? Odds bullets and blades! I'll write a
good bold hand, however.

  Sir Luc. Pray compose yourself.

  Acres. Come — now, shall I begin with an oath?
Do, Sir Lucius, let me begin with a damme.   15

  Sir Luc. Pho! pho! do the thing decently, and
like a Christian. Begin now — *Sir* ——

  Acres. That's too civil by half.

  *Sir Luc. To prevent the confusion that might
arise* ——   20

  Acres. Well ——

  *Sir Luc. From our both addressing the same
lady* ——

  Acres. Ay, there's the reason — *same lady* —
well ——   25

  Sir Luc. I shall expect the honour of your company ——

Acres. Zounds! I'm not asking him to dinner.

Sir Luc. Pray be easy.

Acres. Well then, *honour of your company* ——

Sir Luc. *To settle our pretensions* ——

5   *Acres.* Well.

Sir Luc. Let me see, ay, King's-Mead-Fields°
will do — *in King's-Mead-Fields.*

Acres. So, that's done — Well, I'll fold it up
presently; my own crest — a hand and dagger
10 shall be the seal.

Sir Luc. You see now this little explanation will
put a stop at once to all confusion or misunder-
standing that might arise between you.

Acres. Ay, we fight to prevent any misunder-
15 standing.

Sir Luc. Now, I'll leave you to fix your own
time. Take my advice, and you'll decide it this
evening if you can; then let the worst come of it,
'twill be off your mind to-morrow.

20   *Acres.* Very true.

Sir Luc. So I shall see nothing more of you,
unless it be by letter, till the evening. — I would
do myself the honour to carry your message; but,
to tell you a secret, I believe I shall have just such
25 another affair on my own hands. There is a gay
captain here, who put a jest on me lately, at the

expense of my country, and I only want to fall
in with the gentleman, to call him out.

Acres. By my valour, I should like to see you
fight first! Odds life! I should like to see you
kill him if it was only to get a little lesson.   5

Sir Luc. I shall be very proud of instructing you.
— Well, for the present — but remember now,
when you meet your antagonist, do everything in
a mild and agreeable manner. — Let your courage
be as keen, but at the same time as polished, as 10
your sword.   [*Exeunt severally.*

ACT IV

Scene I. *Acres' Lodgings*

Acres *and* David

Dav. Then, by the mass, sir! I would do no
such thing — ne'er a Sir Lucius O'Trigger in the
kingdom should make me fight, when I wa'n't so
minded. Oons! what will the old lady say when
5 she hears o't?

Acres. Ah! David, if you had heard Sir Lucius!
— Odds sparks and flames! he would have roused
your valour.

Dav. Not he, indeed. I hate such bloodthirsty
10 cormorants. Look'ee, master, if you'd wanted
a bout at boxing, quarter-staff, or short-staff,°
I should never be the man to bid you cry off: but
for your curst sharps and snaps,° I never knew
any good come of 'em.

15 *Acres.* But my honour, David, my honour!
I must be very careful of my honour.

Dav. Ay, by the mass! and I would be very
careful of it; and I think in return my honour
couldn't do less than to be very careful of me.

86

Acres. Odds blades! David, no gentleman will
ever risk the loss of his honour.

Dav. I say then, it would be but civil in honour
never to risk the loss of a gentleman. — Look'ee,
master, this honour seems to me to be a marvel- 5
lous false friend: ay, truly, a very courtier-like
servant. — Put the case, I was a gentleman (which,
thank God, no one can say of me;) well — my
honour makes me quarrel with another gentleman
of my acquaintance. — So — we fight. (Pleasant 10
enough that!) Boh! I kill him — (the more's
my luck!) now, pray who gets the profit of it? —
Why, my honour. But put the case that he kills
me! — by the mass! I go to the worms, and
my honour whips over to my enemy.   15

Acres. No, David — in that case — Odds crowns
and laurels! — your honour follows you to the
grave.

Dav. Now, that's just the place where I could
make a shift to do without it.   20

Acres. Zounds! David, you are a coward! —
It doesn't become my valour to listen to you. —
What, shall I disgrace my ancestors? — Think
of that, David — think what it would be to disgrace
my ancestors!   25

Dav. Under favour, the surest way of not disgrac-

ing them, is to keep as long as you can out of their
company. Look'ee now, master, to go to them
in such haste — with an ounce of lead in your
brains — I should think might as well be let alone.
5 Our ancestors are very good kind of folks; but
they are the last people I should choose to have
a visiting acquaintance with.

Acres. But, David, now, you don't think there is
such very, very, very great danger, hey? — Odds
10 life! people often fight without any mischief done!

Dav. By the mass, I think 'tis ten to one against
you! — Oons! here to meet some lion-headed fellow, I warrant, with his double-barrelled swords,
and cut-and-thrust pistols! — Lord bless us! it
15 makes me tremble to think o't — Those be such
desperate bloody-minded weapons! Well, I never
could abide 'em — from a child I never could
fancy 'em! — I suppose there an't been so merciless
a beast in the world as your loaded pistol!

20   *Acres.* Zounds! I won't be afraid! — Odds fire
and fury! you shan't make me afraid. — Here
is the challenge, and I have sent for my dear friend
Jack Absolute to carry it for me.

Dav. Ay, i' the name of mischief, let him be the
25 messenger. — For my part, I wouldn't lend a hand
to it for the best horse in your stable. By the

mass! it don't look like another letter. It is, as
I may say, a designing and malicious-looking
letter; and I warrant smells of gunpowder like
a soldier's pouch! — Oons! I wouldn't swear it
mayn't go off!   5

Acres. Out, you poltroon! you han't the valour
of a grasshopper.

Dav. Well, I say no more — 'twill be sad news,
to be sure, at Clod-Hall! but I ha' done. — How
Phillis will howl when she hears of it! — Ay, poor 10
bitch, she little thinks what shooting her master's
going after! And I warrant old Crop, who has
carried your honour, field and road, these ten
years, will curse the hour he was born.
                              [*Whimpering.*

Acres. It won't do, David — I am determined 15
to fight — so get along, you coward, while I'm in
the mind.

Enter SERVANT

Ser. Captain Absolute, sir.

Acres. Oh! show him up.   [*Exit* SERVANT.

Dav. Well, Heaven send we be all alive this time 20
to-morrow.

Acres. What's that? — Don't provoke me, David!

Dav. Good-bye, master.   [*Whimpering.*

Acres. Get along, you cowardly, dastardly, croaking raven!   [*Exit* DAVID.

Enter CAPTAIN ABSOLUTE

Abs. What's the matter, Bob?

Acres. A vile, sheep-hearted blockhead! If I
5 hadn't the valour of St. George and the dragon°
to boot ——

Abs. But what did you want with me, Bob?

Acres. Oh! — There —— [*Gives him the challenge.*

Abs. [*Aside.*] *To Ensign Beverley.* — So, what's
10 going on now! — [*Aloud.*] Well, what's this?

Acres. A challenge!

Abs. Indeed! Why, you won't fight him; will you, Bob?

Acres. Egad, but I will, Jack. Sir Lucius has
15 wrought me to it. He has left me full of rage — and I'll fight this evening, that so much good passion mayn't be wasted.

Abs. But what have I to do with this?

Acres. Why, as I think you know something of
20 this fellow, I want you to find him out for me, and give him this mortal defiance.

Abs. Well, give it to me, and trust me he gets it.

Acres. Thank you, my dear friend, my dear Jack; but it is giving you a great deal of trouble.

Abs. Not in the least — I beg you won't mention it. — No trouble in the world I assure you.

Acres. You are very kind. — What it is to have a friend! — You couldn't be my second, could you, Jack?   5

Abs. Why no, Bob — not in this affair — it would not be quite so proper.

Acres. Well, then, I must get my friend Sir Lucius. I shall have your good wishes, however, Jack?   10

Abs. Whenever he meets you, believe me.

Reënter SERVANT

Ser. Sir Anthony Absolute is below, inquiring for the captain.

Abs. I'll come instantly. — [*Exit* SERVANT.] Well, my little hero, success attend you.   [*Going.* 15

Acres. Stay — stay, Jack. — If Beverley should ask you what kind of a man your friend Acres is, do tell him I am a devil of a fellow — will you, Jack?

Abs. To be sure I shall. I'll say you are a determined dog — hey, Bob?   20

Acres. Ay, do, do — and if that frightens him, egad, perhaps he mayn't come. So tell him I generally kill a man a week; will you, Jack?

Abs. I will, I will; I'll say you are called in the country Fighting Bob.

Acres. Right — right — 'tis all to prevent mischief; for I don't want to take his life if I clear 5 my honour.

Abs. No! — that's very kind of you.

Acres. Why, you don't wish me to kill him — do you, Jack?

Abs. No, upon my soul, I do not. But a devil 10 of a fellow, hey?   [*Going.*

Acres. True, true — but stay — stay, Jack — you may add, that you never saw me in such a rage before — a most devouring rage!

Abs. I will, I will.

15 *Acres.* Remember, Jack — a determined dog.

Abs. Ay, ay, Fighting Bob!   [*Exeunt severally.*

SCENE II. *Mrs. Malaprop's Lodgings*

MRS. MALAPROP *and* LYDIA

Mrs. Mal. Why, thou perverse one! — tell me what you can object to him? Isn't he a handsome man? — tell me that. A genteel man? 20 a pretty figure of a man?

Lyd. [*Aside.*] She little thinks whom she is praising! — [*Aloud.*] So is Beverley, ma'am.

Mrs. Mal. No caparisons,° miss, if you please.
Caparisons don't become a young woman. No!
Captain Absolute is indeed a fine gentleman!
　Lyd. Ay, the Captain Absolute you have seen.
[*Aside.*
　Mrs. Mal. Then he's so well bred; — so full of 5
alacrity, and adulation! — and has so much to
say for himself: — in such good language too!
His physiognomy° so grammatical! Then his
presence is so noble! I protest, when I saw him,
I thought of what Hamlet says in the play: —　10
" Hesperian curls° — the front of Job himself! —
　An eye, like March, to threaten at command! —
　A station, like Harry Mercury, new — "
Something about kissing — on a hill — however,
the similitude° struck me directly.　　　15
　Lyd. How enraged she'll be presently, when she
discovers her mistake!　　　　　[*Aside.*

　　　　　　Enter SERVANT

　Ser. Sir Anthony and Captain Absolute are
below, ma'am.
　Mrs. Mal. Show them up here. — [*Exit* SER-
VANT.] Now, Lydia, I insist on your behaving as 20
becomes a young woman. Show your good breeding, at least, though you have forgot your duty.

Lyd. Madam, I have told you my resolution! —
I shall not only give him no encouragement, but
I won't even speak to, or look at him.
[*Flings herself into a chair, with her face from the
door.*

Enter SIR ANTHONY ABSOLUTE *and* CAPTAIN
ABSOLUTE

Sir Anth. Here we are, Mrs. Malaprop; come to
5 mitigate the frowns of unrelenting beauty, — and
difficulty enough I had to bring this fellow. — I
don't know what's the matter; but if I had not
held him by force, he'd have given me the slip.
Mrs. Mal. You have infinite trouble, Sir An-
10 thony, in the affair. I am ashamed for the cause!
— [*Aside to* LYDIA.] Lydia, Lydia, rise, I be-
seech you! — pay your respects!
Sir Anth. I hope, madam, that Miss Languish
has reflected on the worth of this gentleman, and
15 the regard due to her aunt's choice, and my alli-
ance. — [*Aside to* CAPTAIN ABSOLUTE.] Now, Jack,
speak to her.
Abs. [*Aside.*] What the devil shall I do! —
[*Aside to* SIR ANTHONY.] You see, sir, she won't
20 even look at me whilst you are here. I knew she

wouldn't! I told you so. Let me entreat you,
sir, to leave us together!
                [*Seems to expostulate with his father.*
Lyd. [*Aside.*] I wonder I ha'n't heard my aunt
exclaim yet! sure she can't have looked at him!
— perhaps their regimentals are alike, and she is 5
something blind.
Sir Anth. I sáy, sir, I won't stir a foot yet!
Mrs. Mal. I am sorry to say, Sir Anthony, that
my affluence° over my niece is very small. — [*Aside
to* LYDIA.] Turn round, Lydia: I blush for you!   10
Sir Anth. May I not flatter myself, that Miss
Languish will assign what cause of dislike she
can have to my son! — [*Aside to* CAPTAIN ABSO-
LUTE.] Why don't you begin, Jack? — Speak,
you puppy — speak!   15
Mrs. Mal. It is impossible, Sir Anthony, she
can have any. She will not say she has. — [*Aside
to* LYDIA.] Answer, hussy! why don't you answer?
Sir Anth. Then, madam, I trust that a childish
and hasty predilection will be no bar to Jack's 20
happiness. — [*Aside to* CAPTAIN ABSOLUTE.] —
Zounds! sirrah! why don't you speak!
Lyd. [*Aside.*] I think my lover seems as little
inclined to conversation as myself. — How strangely
blind my aunt must be!   25

Abs. Hem! hem! madam — hem! — [*Attempts
to speak, then returns to* SIR ANTHONY.] Faith! sir,
I am so confounded! — and — so — so — confused!
— I told you I should be so, sir — I knew it. —
5 The — the — tremor of my passion entirely takes
away my presence of mind.

Sir Anth. But it don't take away your voice,
fool, does it? — Go up, and speak to her directly!
  [CAPTAIN ABSOLUTE *makes signs to* MRS. MALA-
    PROP *to leave them together.*

Mrs. Mal. Sir Anthony, shall we leave them
10 together? — [*Aside to* LYDIA.] Ah! you stubborn
little vixen!

Sir Anth. Not yet, ma'am, not yet! — [*Aside
to* CAPTAIN ABSOLUTE.] What the devil are you at?
unlock your jaws, sirrah, or ——

15 *Abs.* [*Aside.*] Now Heaven send she may be
too sullen to look round! — I must disguise my
voice. — [*Draws near* LYDIA, *and speaks in a low
hoarse tone.*] Will not Miss Languish lend an ear
to the mild accents of true love? Will not ——

20 *Sir Anth.* What the devil ails the fellow? Why
don't you speak out? — not stand croaking like
a frog in a quinsy!

Abs. The — the — excess of my awe, and my
— my — my modesty, quite choke me!

Sir Anth. Ah! your modesty again! — I'll tell you what, Jack; if you don't speak out directly, and glibly too, I shall be in such a rage! — Mrs. Malaprop, I wish the lady would favour us with something more than a side-front.   5

[MRS. MALAPROP *seems to chide* LYDIA.

Abs. [*Aside.*] So all will out, I see! — [*Goes up to* LYDIA, *speaks softly.*] Be not surprised, my Lydia, suppress all surprise at present.

Lyd. [*Aside.*] Heavens! 'tis Beverley's voice! Sure he can't have imposed on Sir Anthony too! 10 — [*Looks round by degrees, then starts up.*] Is this possible! — my Beverley! — how can this be? — my Beverley?

Abs. Ah! 'tis all over.   [*Aside.*

Sir Anth. Beverley! — the devil — Beverley! 15 — What can the girl mean? — This is my son, Jack Absolute.

Mrs. Mal. For shame, hussy! for shame! your head runs so on that fellow, that you have him always in your eyes! — beg Captain Absolute's 20 pardon directly.

Lyd. I see no Captain Absolute, but my loved Beverley!

Sir Anth. Zounds! the girl's mad! — her brain's turned by reading.   25

H

Mrs. Mal. O' my conscience, I believe so! —
What do you mean by Beverley, hussy? — You
saw Captain Absolute before to-day; there he is
— your husband that shall be.

5   *Lyd.* With all my soul, ma'am — when I refuse
my Beverley ——

Sir Anth. Oh! she's as mad as Bedlam! —
or has this fellow been playing us a rogue's
trick! — Come here, sirrah, who the devil are
10 you?

Abs. Faith, sir, I am not quite clear myself;
but I'll endeavour to recollect.

Sir Anth. Are you my son or not? — answer for
your mother, you dog, if you won't for me.

15   *Mrs. Mal.* Ay, sir, who are you? O mercy!
I begin to suspect! —

Abs. [*Aside.*] Ye powers of impudence, befriend
me! — [*Aloud.*] Sir Anthony, most assuredly I
am your wife's son and that I sincerely believe
20 myself to be yours also, I hope my duty has always
shown. — Mrs. Malaprop, I am your most respect-
ful admirer, and shall be proud to add affectionate
nephew. — I need not tell my Lydia, that she sees
her faithful Beverley, who, knowing the singular
25 generosity of her temper, assumed that name and
station, which has proved a test of the most dis-

interested love, which he now hopes to enjoy in a
more elevated character.

Lyd. So! — there will be no elopement after
all!   [*Sullenly.*

Sir Anth. Upon my soul, Jack, thou art a very 5
impudent fellow! to do you justice, I think I never
saw a piece of more consummate assurance!

Abs. Oh, you flatter me, sir — you compliment
— 'tis my modesty you know, sir, — my modesty
that has stood in my way.   10

Sir Anth. Well, I am glad you are not the dull,
insensible varlet you pretended to be, however!
— I'm glad you have made a fool of your father,
you dog — I am. So this was your *penitence,* your
duty and *obedience!* — I thought it was sudden! — 15
You never heard their names before, not you! —
what, the Languishes of Worcestershire, hey? — *if
you could please me in the affair it was all you desired!* — Ah! you dissembling villain! — What!
— [*Pointing to* Lydia] *she squints, don't she?* — *a* 20
little red-haired girl! — hey? — Why, you hypocritical young rascal! — I wonder you a'n't ashamed
to hold up your head!

Abs. 'Tis with difficulty, sir. — I am confused
— very much confused, as you must perceive.   25

Mrs. Mal. O Lud! Sir Anthony! — a new light

breaks in upon me! — hey! — how! what! captain,
did you write the letters then? — What — am I
to thank you for the elegant compilation° of *an
old weather-beaten she-dragon* — hey! — O mercy!
5 — was it you that reflected on my parts of speech?

Abs. Dear sir! my modesty will be overpowered
at last, if you don't assist me — I shall certainly
not be able to stand it!

Sir Anth. Come, come, Mrs. Malaprop, we must
10 forget and forgive; — odds life! matters have taken
so clever a turn all of a sudden, that I could find
in my heart to be so good-humoured! and so gallant! hey! Mrs. Malaprop!

Mrs. Mal. Well, Sir Anthony, since you desire
15 it, we will not anticipate the past! — so mind,
young people — our retrospection will be all to
the future.

Sir Anth. Come, we must leave them together;
Mrs. Malaprop, they long to fly into each other's
20 arms, I warrant! — Jack — isn't the cheek as I
said, hey? — and the eye, you rogue! — and the
lip — hey? Come, Mrs. Malaprop, we'll not disturb their tenderness — theirs is the time of life
for happiness! — *Youth's the season made for joy* —
25 [*Sings.*] — hey! — Odds life! I'm in such spirits,
— I don't know what I could not do! — Permit

me, ma'am — [*Gives his hand to* MRS. MALAPROP.]
Tol-de-rol — 'gad, I should like to have a little
fooling myself — Tol-de-rol ! de-rol.
   [*Exit, singing and handing* MRS. MALAPROP.—
   LYDIA *sits sullenly in her chair.*
   Abs. [*Aside.*] So much thought bodes me no
good. — [*Aloud.*] So grave, Lydia !   5
   Lyd. Sir !
   Abs. [*Aside.*] So ! — egad ! I thought as much !
— that monosyllable has froze me ! — [*Aloud.*]
What, Lydia, now that we are as happy in our
friends' consent, as in our mutual vows ——   10
   Lyd. Friends' consent indeed !   [*Peevishly.*
   Abs. Come, come, we must lay aside some of
our romance — a little wealth and comfort may
be endured after all. And for your fortune, the
lawyers shall make such settlements as ——   15
   Lyd. Lawyers ! I hate lawyers !
   Abs. Nay, then, we will not wait for their lin-
gering forms, but instantly procure the licence,
and ——
   Lyd. The licence ! — I hate licence !   20
   Abs. Oh my love ! be not so unkind ! — thus
let me entreat ——   [*Kneeling.*
   Lyd. Psha ! — what signifies kneeling, when you
know I must have you ?

Abs. [*Rising.*] Nay, madam, there shall be no
constraint upon your inclinations, I promise you.
— If I have lost your heart, I resign the rest —
[*Aside.*] 'Gad, I must try what a little spirit will
5 do.

Lyd. [*Rising.*] Then, sir, let me tell you, the
interest you had there was acquired by a mean,
unmanly imposition, and deserves the punishment
of fraud. — What, you have been treating me like
10 a child! — humouring my romance! and laughing,
I suppose, at your success!

Abs. You wrong me, Lydia, you wrong me —
only hear ——

Lyd. So, while I fondly imagined we were deceiv-
15 ing my relations, and flattered myself that I should
outwit and incense them all — behold my hopes
are to be crushed at once, by my aunt's consent and
approbation — and I am myself the only dupe at
last! — [*Walking about in a heat.*] But here, sir,
20 here is the picture — Beverley's picture! [*taking
a miniature from her bosom*] which I have worn,
night and day, in spite of threats and entreaties!
— There, sir; [*flings it to him*] and be assured I
throw the original from my heart as easily.

25 *Abs.* Nay, nay, ma'am, we will not differ as to
that. — Here, [*taking out a picture*] here is Miss

Lydia Languish. — What a difference! — ay, there is the heavenly assenting smile that first gave soul and spirit to my hopes! — those are the lips which sealed a vow, as yet scarce dry in Cupid's calendar! and there the half-resentful blush, that would 5 have checked the ardour of my thanks! — Well, all that's past! — all over indeed! — There, madam — in beauty, that copy is not equal to you, but in my mind its merit over the original, in being still the same, is such — that — I can- 10 not find in my heart to part with it.

[*Puts it up again.*

Lyd. [*Softening.*] 'Tis your own doing, sir — I — I — I suppose you are perfectly satisfied.

Abs. O, most certainly — sure, now, this is much better than being in love! — ha! ha! ha! 15 — there's some spirit in this! — What signifies breaking some scores of solemn promises: — all that's of no consequence, you know. — To be sure people will say, that miss don't know her own mind — but never mind that! Or, perhaps, they 20 may be ill-natured enough to hint, that the gentleman grew tired of the lady and forsook her — but don't let that fret you.

Lyd. There is no bearing his insolence.

[*Bursts into tears.*

Reënter MRS. MALAPROP *and* SIR ANTHONY
ABSOLUTE

Mrs. Mal. Come, we must interrupt your billing and cooing awhile.

Lyd. This is worse than your treachery and
deceit, you base ingrate!   [*Sobbing.*

5   *Sir Anth.* What the devil's the matter now! —
Zounds! Mrs. Malaprop, this is the oddest billing
and cooing I ever heard! — but what the deuce is
the meaning of it? — I am quite astonished!

Abs. Ask the lady, sir.

10   *Mrs. Mal.* Oh mercy! — I'm quite analysed,° for
my part! — Why, Lydia, what is the reason of this?

Lyd. Ask the gentleman, ma'am.

Sir Anth. Zounds! I shall be in a frenzy! —
Why, Jack, you are not come out to be any one
15 else, are you?

Mrs. Mal. Ay, sir, there's no more trick, is there?
— you are not like Cerberus, three gentlemen at
once, are you?

Abs. You'll not let me speak — I say the lady
20 can account for this much better than I can.

Lyd. Ma'am, you once commanded me never
to think of Beverley again — there is the man —
I now obey you: for, from this moment, I renounce
him for ever.   [*Exit.*

Mrs. Mal. O mercy! and miracles! what a
turn here is — why sure, captain, you haven't
behaved disrespectfully to my niece.

Sir Anth. Ha! ha! ha! — ha! ha ! ha! — now
I see it. Ha! ha! ha! — now I see it — you 5
have been too lively, Jack.

Abs. Nay, sir, upon my word ——

Sir Anth. Come, no lying, Jack — I'm sure
'twas so.

Mrs. Mal. O Lud! Sir Anthony! — O fy, captain! 10

Abs. Upon my soul, ma'am ——

Sir Anth. Come, no excuses, Jack; why, your
father, you rogue, was so before you: — the blood
of the Absolutes was always impatient. — Ha! ha!
ha! poor little Lydia! why, you've frightened her, 15
you dog, you have.

Abs. By all that's good, sir ——

Sir Anth. Zounds! say no more, I tell you —
Mrs. Malaprop shall make your peace. — You
must make his peace, Mrs. Malaprop: — you must 20
tell her 'tis Jack's way — tell her 'tis all our ways
— it runs in the blood of our family! — Come
away, Jack — Ha! ha! ha! Mrs. Malaprop —
a young villain!   [*Pushing him out.*

Mrs. Mal. O! Sir Anthony! — O fy, captain! 25
                              [*Exeunt severally.*

Scene III. *The North Parade*

Enter Sir Lucius O'Trigger

Sir Luc. I wonder where this Captain Absolute hides himself! Upon my conscience! these officers are always in one's way in love affairs: — I remember I might have married lady Dorothy Carmine, 5 if it had not been for a little rogue of a major, who ran away with her before she could get a sight of me! And I wonder too what it is the ladies can see in them to be so fond of them — unless it be a touch of the old serpent in 'em, that makes the 10 little creatures be caught, like vipers, with a bit of red cloth. Ha! isn't this the captain coming? — faith it is! — There is a probability of succeeding about that fellow, that is mighty provoking! Who is he talking to?   [*Steps aside.*

Enter Captain Absolute

15 *Abs.* [*Aside.*] To what fine purpose I have been plotting! a noble reward for all my schemes, upon my soul! — a little gipsy! — I did not think her romance could have made her so absurd either. 'Sdeath, I never was in a worse humour in my

life! — I could cut my own throat, or any other person's, with the greatest pleasure in the world!

Sir Luc. Oh, faith! I'm in the luck of it. I never could have found him in a sweeter temper for my purpose — to be sure I'm just come in the 5 nick! Now to enter into conversation with him, and so quarrel genteelly. — [*Goes up to* Captain Absolute.] With regard to that matter, captain, I must beg leave to differ in opinion with you.

Abs. Upon my word, then, you must be a very 10 subtle disputant: — because, sir, I happened just then to be giving no opinion at all.

Sir Luc. That's no reason. For give me leave to tell you, a man may think an untruth as well as speak one. 15

Abs. Very true, sir; but if a man never utters his thoughts, I should think they might stand a chance of escaping controversy.

Sir Luc. Then, sir, you differ in opinion with me, which amounts to the same thing. 20

Abs. Hark'ee, Sir Lucius; if I had not before known you to be a gentleman, upon my soul, I should not have discovered it at this interview: for what you can drive at, unless you mean to quarrel with me, I cannot conceive! 25

Sir Luc. I humbly thank you, sir, for the quick-

ness of your apprehension. — [*Bowing.*] You have
named the very thing I would be at.

Abs. Very well, sir; I shall certainly not balk
your inclinations. — But I should be glad you
5 would please to explain your motives.

Sir Luc. Pray sir, be easy; the quarrel is a very
pretty quarrel as it stands; we should only spoil
it by trying to explain it. However, your memory
is very short, or you could not have forgot an affront
10 you passed on me within this week. So, no more,
but name your time and place.

Abs. Well, sir, since you are so bent on it, the
sooner the better; let it be this evening — here,
by the Spring Gardens.° We shall scarcely be
15 interrupted.

Sir Luc. Faith! that same interruption in affairs of this nature shows very great ill-breeding.
I don't know what's the reason, but in England,
if a thing of this kind gets wind, people make such
20 a pother, that a gentleman can never fight in peace
and quietness. However, if it's the same to you,
captain, I should take it as a particular kindness
if you'd let us meet in King's-Mead-Fields, as a
little business will call me there about six o'clock,
25 and I may despatch both matters at once.

Abs. 'Tis the same to me exactly. A little

after six, then, we will discuss this matter more
seriously.

Sir Luc. If you please, sir; there will be very
pretty small-sword light, though it won't do for a
long shot.   So that matter's settled, and my mind's 5
at ease!   [*Exit.*
                    Enter FAULKLAND

Abs. Well met! I was going to look for you.
O Faulkland! all the demons of spite and disappointment have conspired against me! I'm
so vexed, that if I had not the prospect of a re- 10
source in being knocked o' the head by-and-by,
I should scarce have spirits to tell you the cause.

Faulk. What can you mean? — Has Lydia
changed her mind? — I should have thought her
duty and inclination would now have pointed to 15
the same object.

Abs. Ay, just as the eyes do of a person who
squints: when her love-eye was fixed on me, t'other,
her eye of duty, was finely obliqued: but when
duty bid her point that the same way, off t'other 20
turned on a swivel, and secured its retreat with a
frown!

Faulk. But what's the resource you ——

Abs. Oh, to wind up the whole, a good-natured
Irishman here has — [*Mimicking* SIR LUCIUS] — 25

begged leave to have the pleasure of cutting my
throat; and I mean to indulge him — that's all.

Faulk. Prithee, be serious!

Abs. 'Tis fact, upon my soul! Sir Lucius
5 O'Trigger — you know him by sight — for some
affront, which I am sure I never intended, has
obliged me to meet him this evening at six o'clock:
'tis on that account I wished to see you; you must
go with me.

10   *Faulk.* Nay, there must be some mistake, sure.
Sir Lucius shall explain himself, and I dare say
matters may be accommodated. But this evening
did you say? I wish it had been any other time.

Abs. Why? there will be light enough: there
15 will (as Sir Lucius says) be very pretty small-sword
light, though it will not do for a long shot. Confound his long shots!

Faulk. But I am myself a good deal ruffled by
a difference I have had with Julia. My vile tor-
20 menting temper has made me treat her so cruelly,
that I shall not be myself till we are reconciled.

Abs. By Heavens! Faulkland, you don't deserve
her!

Enter SERVANT, *gives* FAULKLAND *a letter, and exit*

Faulk. Oh, Jack! this is from Julia. I dread to
25 open it! I fear it may be to take a last leave! —

perhaps to bid me return her letters, and restore
—— Oh, how I suffer for my folly!

Abs. Here, let me see. — [*Takes the letter and
opens it.*] Ay, a final sentence, indeed! — 'tis all
over with you, faith!   5

Faulk. Nay, Jack, don't keep me in suspense!

Abs. Hear then. — [*Reads.*] *As I am convinced
that my dear Faulkland's own reflections have already upbraided him for his last unkindness to me,
I will not add a word on the subject. I wish to speak* 10
with you as soon as possible. Yours ever and truly,
JULIA. There's stubbornness and resentment for
you! — [*Gives him the letter.*] Why, man, you don't
seem one whit the happier at this!

Faulk. O yes, I am; but — but ——   15

Abs. Confound your buts! you never hear anything that would make another man bless himself,
but you immediately damn it with a but!

Faulk. Now, Jack, as you are my friend, own
honestly — don't you think there is something 20
forward, something indelicate, in this haste to
forgive? Women should never sue for reconciliation: that should always come from us. They
should retain their coldness till wooed to kindness;
and their pardon, like their love, should "not un- 25
sought be won."

Abs. I have not patience to listen to you! thou'rt incorrigible! to say no more on the subject. I must go to settle a few matters. Let me see you before six, remember, at my lodgings. A poor
5 industrious devil like me, who have toiled, and drudged, and plotted to gain my ends, and am at last disappointed by other people's folly, may in pity be allowed to swear and grumble a little; but a captious sceptic in love, a slave to fretfulness
10 and whim, who has no difficulties but of his own creating, is a subject more fit for ridicule than compassion!   [*Exit.*

Faulk. I feel his reproaches; yet I would not change this too exquisite nicety for the gross con-
15 tent with which he tramples on the thorns of love! His engaging me in this duel has started an idea in my head, which I will instantly pursue. I'll use it as the touchstone of Julia's sincerity and disinterestedness. If her love prove pure and
20 sterling ore, my name will rest on it with honour; and once I've stamped it there, I lay aside my doubts for ever! But if the dross of selfishness, the alloy of pride, predominate, 'twill be best to leave her as a toy for some less cautious fool to
25 sigh for!   [*Exit.*

ACT V

Julia *discovered alone*

Jul. How this message has alarmed me! what dreadful accident can he mean? why such charge to be alone? — O Faulkland! — how many unhappy moments — how many tears have you cost me.   5

Enter Faulkland

Jul. What means this? — why this caution, Faulkland?

Faulk. Alas! Julia, I am come to take a long farewell.

Jul. Heavens! what do you mean?   10

Faulk. You see before you a wretch, whose life is forfeited. Nay, start not! — the infirmity of my temper has drawn all this misery on me. I left you fretful and passionate — an untoward accident drew me into a quarrel — the event is, 15 that I must fly this kingdom instantly. O Julia, had I been so fortunate as to have called you mine entirely, before this mischance had fallen on me, I should not so deeply dread my banishment!

ɪ   113

Jul. My soul is oppressed with sorrow at the nature of your misfortune: had these adverse circumstances arisen from a less fatal cause, I should have felt strong comfort in the thought that
5 I could now chase from your bosom every doubt of the warm sincerity of my love. My heart has long known no other guardian — I now entrust my person to your honour — we will fly together. When safe from pursuit, my father's will may be fulfilled —
10 and I receive a legal claim to be the partner of your sorrows, and tenderest comforter. Then on the bosom of your wedded Julia, you may lull your keen regret to slumbering; while virtuous love, with a cherub's hand, shall smooth the brow of upbraiding
15 thought, and pluck the thorn from compunction.

Faulk. O Julia! I am bankrupt in gratitude! but the time is so pressing, it calls on you for so hasty a resolution! — Would you not wish some hours to weigh the advantages you forego, and
20 what little compensation poor Faulkland can make you beside his solitary love?

Jul. I ask not a moment. No, Faulkland, I have loved you for yourself: and if I now, more than ever, prize the solemn engagement which so
25 long has pledged us to each other, it is because it leaves no room for hard aspersions on my fame, and

puts the seal of duty to an act of love. But let
us not linger. Perhaps this delay ——

Faulk. 'Twill be better I should not venture out
again till dark. Yet am I grieved to think what
numberless distresses will press heavy on your gentle 5
disposition!

Jul. Perhaps your fortune may be forfeited by
this unhappy act. I know not whether 'tis so; but
sure that alone can never make us unhappy. The
little I have will be sufficient to support us; and 10
exile never should be splendid.

Faulk. Ay, but in such an abject state of life,
my wounded pride perhaps may increase the natural
fretfulness of my temper, till I become a rude,
morose companion, beyond your patience to endure. 15
Perhaps the recollection of a deed my conscience
cannot justify may haunt me in such gloomy and
unsocial fits, that I shall hate the tenderness that
would relieve me, break from your arms, and
quarrel with your fondness!   20

Jul. If your thoughts should assume so unhappy
a bent, you will the more want some mild and
affectionate spirit to watch over and console you:
one who, by bearing your infirmities with gentleness
and resignation, may teach you so to bear the evils 25
of your fortune,

Faulk. Julia, I have proved you to the quick! and with this useless device I throw away all my doubts. How shall I plead to be forgiven this last unworthy effect of my restless, unsatisfied disposi-
5 tion?

Jul. Has no such disaster happened as you related?

Faulk. I am ashamed to own that it was pretended; yet in pity, Julia, do not kill me with re-
10 senting a fault which never can be repeated: but sealing, this once, my pardon, let me to-morrow, in the face of Heaven, receive my future guide and monitress, and expiate my past folly by years of tender adoration.

15   *Jul.* Hold, Faulkland! — that you are free from a crime, which I before feared to name, Heaven knows how sincerely I rejoice! These are tears of thankfulness for that! But that your cruel doubts should have urged you to an imposition that has
20 wrung my heart, gives me now a pang more keen than I can express!

Faulk. By Heavens! Julia ——

Jul. Yet hear me. — My father loved you, Faulkland! and you preserved the life that tender parent
25 gave me; in his presence I pledged my hand — joyfully pledged it — where before I had given my

heart. When, soon after, I lost that parent, it
seemed to me that Providence had, in Faulkland,
shown me whither to transfer without a pause, my
grateful duty, as well as my affection: hence I
have been content to bear from you what pride and 5
delicacy would have forbid me from another. I
will not upbraid you, by repeating how you have
trifled with my sincerity ——

Faulk. I confess it all! yet hear —— .

Jul. After such a year of trial, I might have 10
flattered myself that I should not have been insulted with a new probation of my sincerity, as
cruel as unnecessary! I now see it is not in your
nature to be content or confident in love. With
this conviction — I never will be yours. While 15
I had hopes that my persevering attention, and
unreproaching kindness, might in time reform
your temper, I should have been happy to have
gained a dearer influence over you; but I will not
furnish you with a licensed power to keep alive an 20
incorrigible fault, at the expense of one who never
would contend with you.

Faulk. Nay, but, Julia, by my soul and honour,
.if after this ——

Jul. But one word more. — As my faith has once 25
been given to you, I never will barter it with another.

I shall pray for your happiness with the truest sincerity; and the dearest blessing I can ask of Heaven
to send you will be to charm you from that unhappy
temper, which alone has prevented the performance
5 of our solemn engagement.   All I request of you is,
that you will yourself reflect upon this infirmity,
and when you number up the many true delights
it has deprived you of, let it not be your least regret,
that it lost you the love of one who would have
10 followed you in beggary through the world!

[Exit.

Faulk. She's gone — for ever! — There was an
awful resolution in her manner, that riveted me
to my place. — O fool! — dolt! — barbarian!
Cursed as I am, with more imperfections than my
15 fellow-wretches, kind Fortune sent a heaven-gifted
cherub to my aid, and, like a ruffian, I have driven
her from my side! — I must now haste to my
appointment.   Well, my mind is tuned for such a
scene.   I shall wish only to become a principal in
20 it, and reverse the tale my cursed folly put me upon
forging here. — O Love! — tormentor! — fiend! —
whose influence, like the moon's, acting on men of
dull souls, makes idiots of them, but meeting subtler
spirits, betrays their course, and urges sensibility
25 to madness!   [Exit.

Enter Lydia *and* Maid

Maid. My mistress, ma'am, I know, was here
just now — perhaps she is only in the next room.
                                              [*Exit.*
Lyd. Heigh-ho! Though he has used me so,
this fellow runs strangely in my head. I believe
one lecture from my grave cousin will make me 5
recall him. [*Reënter* Julia.] O Julia, I am come to
you with such an appetite for consolation. — Lud!
child, what's the matter with you? You have
been crying! — I'll be hanged if that Faulkland
has not been tormenting you!   10
Jul. You mistake the cause of my uneasiness! —
Something has flurried me a little. Nothing that
you can guess at. — [*Aside.*] I would not accuse
Faulkland to a sister!
Lyd. Ah! whatever vexations you may have, I 15
can assure you mine surpass them. You know
who Beverley proves to be?
Jul. I will now own to you, Lydia, that Mr.
Faulkland had before informed me of the whole
affair. Had young Absolute been the person you 20
took him for, I should not have accepted your confidence on the subject, without a serious endeavour
to counteract your caprice.

Lyd. So, then, I see I have been deceived by everyone! But I don't care — I'll never have him.

Jul. Nay, Lydia ——

Lyd. Why, is it not provoking? when I thought
5 we were coming to the prettiest distress imaginable, to find myself made a mere Smithfield bargain of at last! There had I projected one of the most sentimental elopements! — so becoming a disguise! — so amiable a ladder of ropes° ! — conscious
10 moon — four horses — Scotch parson — with such surprise to Mrs. Malaprop — and such paragraphs in the newspapers! — Oh, I shall die with disappointment!

Jul. I don't wonder at it!

15 *Lyd.* Now — sad reverse! — what have I to expect, but, after a deal of flimsy preparation with a bishop's licence, and my aunt's blessing, to go simpering up to the altar; or perhaps be cried three times in a country church, and have an unmannerly
20 fat clerk ask the consent of every butcher in the parish to join John Absolute and Lydia Languish, spinster! Oh, that I should live to hear myself called spinster!

Jul. Melancholy indeed!

25 *Lyd.* How mortifying, to remember the dear delicious shifts I used to be put to, to gain half a

minute's conversation with this fellow! How often
have I stole forth, in the coldest night in January,
and found him in the garden, stuck like a dripping
statue! There would he kneel to me in the snow,
and sneeze and cough so pathetically! he shivering 5
with cold and I with apprehension! and while
the freezing blast numbed our joints, how warmly
would he press me to pity his flame, and glow with
mutual ardour! — Ah, Julia, that was something
like being in love.   10

Jul. If I were in spirits, Lydia, I should chide
you only by laughing heartily at you; but it suits
more the situation of my mind, at present, earnestly
to entreat you not to let a man, who loves you with
sincerity, suffer that unhappiness from your caprice, 15
which I know too well caprice can inflict.

Lyd. O Lud! what has brought my aunt here?

Enter MRS. MALAPROP, FAG, *and* DAVID

Mrs. Mal. So! so! here's fine work! — here's
fine suicide, parricide, and simulation,° going on in
the fields! and Sir Anthony not to be found to 20
prevent the antistrophe°!

Jul. For Heaven's sake, madam, what's the
meaning of this?

Mrs. Mal. That gentleman can tell you — 'twas he enveloped the affair to me.

Lyd. Do, sir, will you, inform us?		[*To* FAG.

Fag. Ma'am, I should hold myself very deficient
5 in every requisite that forms the man of breeding, if I delayed a moment to give all the information in my power to a lady so deeply interested in the affair as you are.

Lyd. But quick! quick, sir!

10 *Fag.* True, ma'am, as you say, one should be quick in divulging matters of this nature; for should we be tedious, perhaps while we are flourishing on the subject, two or three lives may be lost!

Lyd. O patience! — Do, ma'am, for Heaven's
15 sake! tell us what is the matter?

Mrs. Mal. Why, murder's the matter! slaughter's the matter! killing's the matter! — but he can tell you the perpendiculars.°

Lyd. Then, prithee, sir, be brief.

20 *Fag.* Why then, ma'am, as to murder — I cannot take upon me to say — and as to slaughter, or manslaughter, that will be as the jury finds it.

Lyd. But who, sir — who are engaged in this?

Fag. Faith, ma'am, one is a young gentleman
25 whom I should be very sorry any thing was to happen to — a very pretty behaved gentleman!

We have lived much together, and always on terms.

Lyd. But who is this? who! who! who?

Fag. My master, ma'am — my master — I speak of my master.

Lyd. Heavens! What, Captain Absolute!   5

Mrs. Mal. Oh, to be sure, you are frightened now!

Jul. But who are with him, sir?

Fag. As to the rest, ma'am, this gentleman can inform you better than I.

Jul. Do speak, friend.   [*To* DAVID. 10

Dav. Look'ee, my lady — by the mass! there's mischief going on. Folks don't use to meet for amusement with firearms, firelocks, fire-engines, fire-screens, fire-office, and the devil knows what other crackers beside! — This, my lady, I say, has 15 an angry favour.°

Jul. But who is there beside Captain Absolute, friend?

Dav. My poor master — under favour for mentioning him first. You know me, my lady — I am 20 David — and my master of course is, or was, Squire Acres. Then comes Squire Faulkland.

Jul. Do, ma'am, let us instantly endeavour to prevent mischief.

Mrs. Mal. O fy! — it would be very inelegant 25 in us: — we should only participate° things.

Dav. Ah! do, Mrs. Aunt, save a few lives — they are desperately given, believe me. — Above all, there is that bloodthirsty Philistine, Sir Lucius O'Trigger.

5 *Mrs. Mal.* Sir Lucius O'Trigger? O mercy! have they drawn poor little dear Sir Lucius into the scrape? — Why, how you stand, girl! you have no more feeling than one of the Derbyshire putri-factions°!

10 *Lyd.* What are we to do, madam?

Mrs. Mal. Why fly with the utmost felicity, to be sure, to prevent mischief! — Here, friend, you can show us the place?

Fag. If you please, ma'am, I will conduct you. — 15 David, do you look for Sir Anthony. [*Exit* DAVID.

Mrs. Mal. Come, girls! this gentleman will exhort° us. — Come, sir, you're our envoy° — lead the way, and we'll precede.

Fag. Not a step before the ladies for the 20 world!

Mrs. Mal. You're sure you know the spot?

Fag. I think I can find it, ma'am; and one good thing is, we shall hear the report of the pistols as we draw near, so we can't well miss 25 them; — never fear, ma'am, never fear.

[*Exeunt, he talking.*

SCENE II.   *The South Parade*

Enter CAPTAIN ABSOLUTE, *putting his sword under
his great coat*

Abs. A sword seen in the streets of Bath would
raise as great an alarm as a mad dog. — How provoking this is in Faulkland! — never punctual!
I shall be obliged to go without him at last. — Oh,
here's Sir Anthony! how shall I escape him?   5
   [*Muffles up his face, and takes a circle to go off.*

Enter SIR ANTHONY ABSOLUTE

Sir Anth. How one may be deceived at a little
distance! only that I see he don't know me, I
could have sworn that was Jack! — Hey! Gad's
life! it is. — Why, Jack, what are you afraid of?
hey! — sure I'm right. — Why Jack, Jack Absolute! 10
                             [*Goes up to him.*
Abs. Really, sir, you have the advantage of me:
— I don't remember ever to have had the honour —
my name is Saunderson, at your service.
Sir Anth. Sir, I beg your pardon — I took you —
hey? — why, zounds! it is — Stay — [*Looks up* 15
to his face.] So, so — your humble servant, Mr.

Saunderson! Why, you scoundrel, what tricks
are you after now?

Abs. Oh, a joke, sir, a joke! I came here on
purpose to look for you, sir.

5   *Sir Anth.* You did! well, I am glad you were so
lucky: — but what are you muffled up so for? —
what's this for? — hey!

Abs. 'Tis cool, sir; isn't? — rather chilly somehow; — but I shall be late — I have a particular
10 engagement.

Sir Anth. Stay! — Why, I thought you were
looking for me? — Pray, Jack, where is't you are
going?

Abs. Going, sir!

15   *Sir Anth.* Ay, where are you going?

Abs. Where am I going?

Sir Anth. You unmannerly puppy!

Abs. I was going, sir, to — to — to — to Lydia
— sir, to Lydia — to make matters up if I could; —
20 and I was looking for you, sir, to — to —

Sir Anth. To go with you, I suppose. — Well,
come along.

Abs. Oh! zounds! no, sir, not for the world! —
I wished to meet with you, sir, — to — to — to —
25 You find it cool, I'm sure, sir — you'd better not
stay out.

Sir Anth. Cool! — not at all. — Well, Jack —
and what will you say to Lydia?

Abs. Oh, sir, beg her pardon, humour her —
promise and vow: but I detain you, sir — consider
the cold air on your gout.   5

Sir Anth. Oh, not at all! — not at all! I'm in
no hurry. — Ah! Jack, you youngsters, when once
you are wounded here [*Putting his hand to* CAPTAIN
ABSOLUTE'S *breast.*] Hey! what the deuce have you
got here?   10

Abs. Nothing, sir — nothing.

Sir Anth. What's this? — here's something hard.

Abs. Oh, trinkets, sir! trinkets! — a bauble for
Lydia!

Sir Anth. Nay, let me see your taste. — [*Pulls* 15
his coat open, the sword falls.] Trinkets! — a bauble
for Lydia! — Zounds! sirrah, you are not going
to cut her throat, are you?

Abs. Ha! ha! ha! — I thought it would divert
you, sir, though I didn't mean to tell you till after- 20
wards.

Sir Anth. You didn't? — Yes, this is a very
diverting trinket, truly!

Abs. Sir, I'll explain to you. — You know, sir,
Lydia is romantic, devilish romantic, and very 25
absurd of course: now, sir, I intend, if she refuses

to forgive me, to unsheath this sword, and swear I'll
fall upon its point, and expire at her feet!

Sir Anth. Fall upon a fiddlestick's end! — why, I
suppose it is the very thing that would please her. —
5 Get along, you fool!

Abs. Well, sir, you shall hear of my success —
you shall hear. — *O Lydia! — forgive me, or this
pointed steel* — says I.

Sir Anth. O, *booby! stab away and welcome* —
10 says she. — Get along! [*Exit* CAPTAIN ABSOLUTE.

Enter DAVID, *running*

Dav. Stop him! stop him! Murder! Thief!
Fire! — Stop fire! Stop fire! — O Sir Anthony —
call! call! bid'm stop! Murder! Fire!

Sir Anth. Fire! Murder! — Where?

15 *Dav.* Oons! he's out of sight! and I'm out of
breath, for my part! O Sir Anthony, why didn't
you stop him? why didn't you stop him?

Sir Anth. Zounds! the fellow's mad! — Stop
whom? stop Jack?

20 *Dav.* Ay, the captain, sir! — there's murder and
slaughter ——

Sir Anth. Murder!

Dav. Ay, please you, Sir Anthony, there's all

kinds of murder, all sorts of slaughter to be seen in
the fields: there's fighting going on, sir — bloody
sword-and-gun fighting!

Sir Anth. Who are going to fight, dunce?

Dav. Every body that I know of, Sir Anthony: 5
— every body is going to fight, my poor master,
Sir Lucius O'Trigger, your son, the captain ——

Sir Anth. Oh, the dog! I see his tricks. — Do you
know the place?

Dav. King's-Mead-Fields.   10

Sir Anth. You know the way?

Dav. Not an inch; but I'll call the mayor —
aldermen — constables — churchwardens — and
beadles — we can't be too many to part them.

Sir Anth. Come along — give me your shoulder! 15
we'll get assistance as we go — the lying villain!
— Well, I shall be in such a frenzy! — So — this
was the history of his trinkets! I'll bauble him!

[*Exeunt.*

SCENE III.   *King's-Mead-Fields*

Enter SIR LUCIUS O'TRIGGER *and* ACRES, *with pistols*

Acres. By my valour! then, Sir Lucius, forty
yards is a good distance. Odds levels and aims! — 20
I say it is a good distance.

K

Sir Luc. Is it for muskets or small field-pieces? Upon my conscience, Mr. Acres, you must leave those things to me. — Stay now — I'll show you. — [*Measures paces along the stage.*] There now, that 5 is a very pretty distance — a pretty gentleman's distance.

Acres. Zounds! we might as well fight in a sentry-box! I tell you, Sir Lucius, the farther he is off, the cooler I shall take my aim.

10 *Sir Luc.* Faith! then I suppose you would aim at him best of all if he was out of sight!

Acres. No, Sir Lucius; but I should think forty or eight-and-thirty yards ——

Sir Luc. Pho! pho! nonsense! three or four 15 feet between the mouths of your pistols is as good as a mile.

Acres. Odds bullets, no! — by my valour! there is no merit in killing him so near: do, my dear Sir Lucius, let me bring him down at a long shot: — 20 a long shot, Sir Lucius, if you love me!

Sir Luc. Well, the gentleman's friend and I must settle that. — But tell me now, Mr. Acres, in case of an accident, is there any little will or commission I could execute for you?

25 *Acres.* I am much obliged to you, Sir Lucius — but I don't understand ——

Sir Luc. Why, you may think there's no being shot at without a little risk — and if an unlucky bullet should carry a quietus with it — I say it will be no time then to be bothering you about family matters.   5

Acres. A quietus!

Sir Luc. For instance, now — if that should be the case — would you choose to be pickled and sent home? — or would it be the same to you to lie here in the Abbey°? — I'm told there is very snug 10 lying in the Abbey.

Acres. Pickled! — Snug lying in the Abbey! — Odds tremors! Sir Lucius, don't talk so!

Sir Luc. I suppose, Mr. Acres, you never were engaged in an affair of this kind before?   15

Acres. No, Sir Lucius, never before.

Sir Luc. Ah! that's a pity! — there's nothing like being used to a thing. — Pray now, how would you receive the gentleman's shot?

Acres. Odds files! — I've practised that — there, 20 Sir Lucius — there. — [*Puts himself in an attitude.*] A side-front, hey? Odd! I'll make myself small enough: I'll stand edgeways.

Sir Luc. Now — you're quite out —for if you stand so when I take my aim ——   25

[*Levelling at him.*

Acres. Zounds! Sir Lucius — are you sure it is not cocked?

Sir Luc. Never fear.

Acres. But — but — you don't know — it may
5 go off of its own head!

Sir Luc. Pho! be easy. — Well, now if I hit you in the body, my bullet has a double chance — for if it misses a vital part of your right side —'twill be very hard if it don't succeed on the left!

10   *Acres.* A vital part?

Sir Luc. But, there — fix yourself so — [*Placing him.*] — let him see the broad-side of your full front — there — now a ball or two may pass clean through your body, and never do any harm
15 at all.

Acres. Clean through me! — a ball or two clean through me!

Sir Luc. Ay, may they — and it is much the genteelest attitude into the bargain.

20   *Acres.* Look'ee! Sir Lucius — I'd just as lieve be shot in an awkward posture as a genteel one; so, by my valour! I will stand edgeways.

Sir Luc. [*Looking at his watch.*] Sure they don't mean to disappoint us — Hah! — no, faith — I
25 think I see them coming.

Acres. Hey! — what! — coming! ——

Sir Luc. Ay. — Who are those yonder getting over the stile?

Acres. There are two of them indeed! — well — let them come — hey, Sir Lucius! — we — we — we — we — won't run.   5

Sir Luc. Run!

Acres. No — I say — we won't run, by my valour!

Sir Luc. What the devil's the matter with you?

Acres. Nothing — nothing — my dear friend — my dear Sir Lucius — but I — I — I don't feel quite 10 so bold, somehow, as I did.

Sir Luc. O fy! — consider your honour.

Acres. Ay — true — my honour. Do, Sir Lucius, edge in a word or two every now and then about my honour.   15

Sir Luc. Well, here they're coming.   [*Looking.*

Acres. Sir Lucius — if I wa'n't with you, I should almost think I was afraid. — If my valour should leave me! — Valour will come and go.

Sir Luc. Then pray keep it fast, while you have it. 20

Acres. Sir Lucius — I doubt it is going — yes — my valour is certainly going! — it is sneaking off! — I feel it oozing out as it were at the palms of my hands!

Sir Luc. Your honour — your honour! — Here 25 they are.

Acres. O mercy! — now — that I was safe at Clod-Hall! or could be shot before I was aware!

Enter FAULKLAND *and* CAPTAIN ABSOLUTE

Sir Luc. Gentlemen, your most obedient. — Hah! — what, Captain Absolute! — So, I suppose, sir, 5 you are come here, just like myself — to do a kind office, first for your friend — then to proceed to business on your own account.

Acres. What, Jack! — my dear Jack! — my dear friend!

10   *Abs.* Hark'ee, Bob, Beverley's at hand.

Sir Luc. Well, Mr. Acres — I don't blame your saluting the gentleman civilly. — [*To* FAULKLAND.] So, Mr. Beverley, if you'll choose your weapons, the captain and I will measure the ground.

15   *Faulk.* My weapons, sir!

Acres. Odds life! Sir Lucius, I'm not going to fight Mr. Faulkland; these are my particular friends.

Sir Luc. What, sir, did you not come here to fight Mr. Acres?

20   *Faulk.* Not I, upon my word, sir.

Sir Luc. Well, now, that's mighty provoking! But I hope, Mr. Faulkland, as there are three of us come on purpose for the game, you won't be so cantankerous as to spoil the party by sitting out.

Abs. O pray, Faulkland, fight to oblige Sir Lucius.

Faulk. Nay, if Mr. Acres is so bent on the matter ——

Acres. No, no, Mr. Faulkland; — I'll bear my disappointment like a Christian. — Look'ee, Sir 5 Lucius, there's no occasion at all for me to fight; and if it is the same to you, I'd as lieve let it alone.

Sir Luc. Observe me, Mr. Acres — I must not be trifled with. You have certainly challenged somebody — and you came here to fight him. Now, 10 if that gentleman is willing to represent him, I can't see, for my soul, why it isn't just the same thing.

Acres. Why no — Sir Lucius — I tell you, 'tis one Beverley I've challenged — a fellow, you see, that dare not show his face! — If he were here, I'd 15 make him give up his pretensions directly!

Abs. Hold, Bob — let me set you right — there is no such man as Beverley in the case. — The person who assumed that name is before you; and as his pretensions are the same in both characters, he is 20 ready to support them in whatever way you please.

Sir Luc. Well, this is lucky. — Now you have an opportunity ——

Acres. What, quarrel with my dear friend Jack Absolute? — not if he were fifty Beverleys! Zounds! 25 Sir Lucius, you would not have me so unnatural.

Sir Luc. Upon my conscience, Mr. Acres, your valour has oozed away with a vengeance!

Acres. Not in the least! Odds backs and abettors! I'll be your second with all my heart — and
5 if you should get a quietus, you may command me entirely. I'll get you snug lying in the Abbey° here; or pickle you, and send you over to Blunderbuss-hall, or any thing of the kind, with the greatest pleasure.

Sir Luc. Pho! pho! you are little better than a
10 coward.

Acres. Mind, gentlemen, he calls me a coward; coward was the word, by my valour!

Sir Luc. Well, sir?

Acres. Look'ee, Sir Lucius, 'tisn't that I mind the
15 word coward — coward may be said in joke — but if you had called me a poltroon, odds daggers and balls ——

Sir Luc. Well, sir?

Acres. I should have thought you a very ill-bred
20 man.

Sir Luc. Pho! you are beneath my notice.

Abs. Nay, Sir Lucius, you can't have a better second than my friend Acres. — He is a most determined dog — called in the country, Fighting
25 Bob. — He generally kills a man a week — don't you, Bob?

Acres. Ay — at home!

Sir Luc. Well, then, captain, 'tis we must begin —
so come out, my little counsellor — [*Draws his sword*]
— and ask the gentleman, whether he will resign the
lady, without forcing you to proceed against him? 5

Abs. Come on then, sir — [*Draws*]; since you
won't let it be an amicable suit, here's my reply.

Enter SIR ANTHONY ABSOLUTE, DAVID, MRS. MALA-
PROP, LYDIA, *and* JULIA

Dav. Knock 'em all down, sweet Sir Anthony;
knock down my master in particular; and bind his
hands over to their good behaviour!   10

Sir Anth. Put up, Jack, put up, or I shall be in
a frenzy — how came you in a duel, sir?

Abs. Faith, sir, that gentleman can tell you better
than I; 'twas he called on me, and you know, sir,
I serve his majesty.   15

Sir Anth. Here's a pretty fellow; I catch him
going to cut a man's throat, and he tells me, he
serves his majesty! — Zounds! sirrah, then how
durst you draw the king's sword against one of his
subjects?   20

Abs. Sir, I tell you! that gentleman called me
out, without explaining his reasons.

Sir Anth. Gad! sir, how came you to call my son out, without explaining your reasons?

Sir Luc. Your son, sir, insulted me in a manner which my honour could not brook.

5 *Sir Anth.* Zounds! Jack, how durst you insult the gentleman in a manner which his honour could not brook?

Mrs. Mal. Come, come, let's have no honour before ladies. — Captain Absolute, come here — How 10 could you intimidate us so? — Here's Lydia has been terrified to death for you.

Abs. For fear I should be killed, or escape, ma'am?

Mrs. Mal. Nay, no delusions to the past — Lydia is convinced; speak, child.

15 *Sir Luc.* With your leave, ma'am, I must put in a word here: I believe I could interpret the young lady's silence. Now mark ——

Lyd. What is it you mean, sir?

Sir Luc. Come, come, Delia, we must be serious 20 now — this is no time for trifling.

Lyd. 'Tis true, sir; and your reproof bids me offer this gentleman my hand, and solicit the return of his affections.

Abs. O! my little angel, say you so! — Sir 25 Lucius — I perceive there must be some mistake here, with regard to the affront which you affirm I

have given you. I can only say, that it could not
have been intentional. And as you must be convinced, that I should not fear to support a real injury, you shall now see that I am not ashamed to
atone for an inadvertency — I ask your pardon. — 5
But for this lady, while honoured with her approbation, I will support my claim against any man
whatever.

Sir Anth. Well said, Jack, and I'll stand by you,
my boy.   10

Acres. Mind, I give up all my claim — I make no
pretensions to any thing in the world; and if I can't
get a wife without fighting for her, by my valour!
I'll live a bachelor.

Sir Luc. Captain, give me your hand: an affront 15
handsomely acknowledged becomes an obligation;
and as for the lady, if she chooses to deny her own
hand-writing, here ——   *[Takes out letters.'*

Mrs. Mal. O, he will dissolve° my mystery! —
Sir Lucius, perhaps there's some mistake — perhaps 20
I can illuminate° ——

Sir Luc. Pray, old gentlewoman, don't interfere
where you have no business. — Miss Languish, are
you my Delia, or not?

Lyd. Indeed, Sir Lucius, I am not.   25
     [Walks aside with CAPTAIN ABSOLUTE.

Mrs. Mal. Sir Lucius O'Trigger — ungrateful as
you are — I own the soft impeachment — pardon
my blushes, I am Delia.

Sir Luc. You Delia — pho! pho! be easy.

5   *Mrs. Mal.* Why, thou barbarous Vandyke° —
those letters are mine — When you are more sensible of my benignity — perhaps I may be brought
to encourage your addresses.

Sir Luc. Mrs. Malaprop, I am extremely sensible
10 of your condescension; and whether you or Lucy
have put this trick on me, I am equally beholden to
you. — And, to show you I am not ungrateful,
Captain Absolute, since you have taken that lady
from me, I'll give you my Delia into the bargain.

15   *Abs.* I am much obliged to you, Sir Lucius; but
here's my friend, Fighting Bob, unprovided for.

Sir Luc. Hah! little Valour — here, will you make
your fortune?

Acres. Odds wrinkles! No. — But give me your
20 hand, Sir Lucius, forget and forgive; but if ever I
give you a chance of pickling me again, say Bob
Acres is a dunce, that's all.

Sir Anth. Come, Mrs. Malaprop, don't be cast
down — you are in your bloom yet.

25   *Mrs. Mal.* O Sir Anthony — men are all bar-
barians.   [*All retire but* JULIA *and* FAULKLAND.

Jul. [*Aside.*] He seems dejected and unhappy —
not sullen; there was some foundation, however,
for the tale he told me — O woman! how true
should be your judgment, when your resolution is so
weak!   5

Faulk. Julia! — how can I sue for what I so little
deserve? I dare not presume — yet Hope is the
child of Penitence.

Jul. O! Faulkland, you have not been more faulty
in your unkind treatment of me, than I am now in 10
wanting inclination to resent it. As my heart
honestly bids me place my weakness to the account
of love, I should be ungenerous not to admit the
same plea for yours.

Faulk. Now I shall be blest indeed!   15

Sir Anth. [*Coming forward.*] What's going on
here? — So you have been quarrelling too, I warrant! Come, Julia, I never interfered before; but
let me have a hand in the matter at last. — All the
faults I have ever seen in my friend Faulkland 20
seemed to proceed from what he calls the delicacy
and warmth of his affection for you — There, marry
him directly, Julia; you'll find he'll mend surprisingly!   [*The rest come forward.*

Sir Luc. Come, now, I hope there is no dissatis- 25
fied person, but what is content; for as I have been

disappointed myself, it will be very hard if I have not
the satisfaction of seeing other people succeed better.

Acres. You are right, Sir Lucius. — So Jack, I
wish you joy — Mr. Faulkland the same. — Ladies,
5 — come now, to show you I'm neither vexed nor
angry, odds tabors and pipes! I'll order the fiddles
in half an hour to the New Rooms° — and I insist
on your all meeting me there.

Sir Anth. 'Gad! sir, I like your spirit; and at
10 night we single lads will drink a health to the young
couples, and a husband to Mrs. Malaprop.

Faulk. Our partners are stolen from us, Jack — I
hope to be congratulated by each other — yours
for having checked in time the errors of an ill-directed
15 imagination, which might have betrayed an innocent
heart; and mine, for having, by her gentleness and
candour, reformed the unhappy temper of one, who
by it made wretched whom he loved most, and tor-
tured the heart he ought to have adored.

20 *Abs.* Well, Jack, we have both tasted the bitters,
as well as the sweets of love; with this difference
only, that you always prepared the bitter cup for
yourself, while I ——

Lyd. Was always obliged to me for it, hey! Mr.
25 Modesty? —— But, come, no more of that — our
happiness is now as unalloyed as general.

Jul. Then let us study to preserve it so: and while
Hope pictures to us a flattering scene of future bliss,
let us deny its pencil those colours which are too
bright to be lasting. — When hearts deserving happiness would unite their fortunes, Virtue would crown 5
them with an unfading garland of modest hurt-
less flowers; but ill-judging Passion will force the
gaudier rose into the wreath, whose thorn offends
them when its leaves are dropped!

[*Exeunt omnes.*

EPILOGUE

BY THE AUTHOR

SPOKEN BY MRS. BULKLEY

Ladies, for you — I heard our poet say —
He'd try to coax some moral from his play:
"One moral's plain," cried I, "without more fuss;
Man's social happiness all rests on us:
5 Through all the drama — whether damned or not —
Love gilds the scene, and women guide the plot.
From every rank obedience is our due —
D'ye doubt? — The world's great stage shall prove
    it true.
The cit, well skilled to shun domestic strife,
10 Will sup abroad; but first he'll ask his wife:
John Trot, his friend, for once will do the same,
But then — he'll just step home to tell his dame.
The surly squire at noon resolves to rule,
And half the day — Zounds! madam is a fool!
15 Convinced at night, the vanquished victor says,
Ah, Kate! you women have such coaxing ways.
The jolly toper chides each tardy blade,
Till reeling Bacchus calls on Love for aid:

144

Then with each toast he sees fair bumpers swim,
And kisses Chloe on the sparkling brim!
  Nay, I have heard that statesmen — great and
    wise —
Will sometimes counsel with a lady's eyes!
The servile suitors watch her various face,   5
She smiles preferment, or she frowns disgrace,
Curtsies a pension here — there nods a place.
  Nor with less awe, in scenes of humbler life,
Is viewed the mistress, or is heard the wife.
The poorest peasant of the poorest soil,   10
The child of poverty, and heir to toil,
Early from radiant Love's impartial light
Steals one small spark to cheer this world of night:
Dear spark! that oft through winter's chilling woes
Is all the warmth his little cottage knows!   15
  The wandering tar, who not for years has pressed
The widowed partner of his day of rest,
On the cold deck, far from her arms removed,
Still hums the ditty which his Susan loved;
And while around the cadence rude is blown,   20
·The boatswain whistles in a softer tone.
  The soldier, fairly proud of wounds and toil,
Pants for the triumph of his Nancy's smile;
But ere the battle should he list her cries,
The lover trembles — and the hero dies!   25

    L

That heart, by war and honour steeled to fear,
Droops on a sigh, and sickens at a tear!
   But ye more cautious, ye nice-judging few,
Who give to beauty only beauty's due,
5 Though friends to love — ye view with deep regret
Our conquests marred, our triumphs incomplete,
Till polished wit more lasting charms disclose,
And judgment fix the darts which beauty throws!
In female breasts did sense and merit rule,
10 The lover's mind would ask no other school;
Shamed into sense, the scholars of our eyes,
Our beaux from gallantry would soon be wise;
Would gladly light, their homage to improve,
The lamp of knowledge at the torch of love!

THE SCHOOL FOR SCANDAL

A PORTRAIT

ADDRESSED TO MRS. CREWE,° WITH THE COMEDY
OF THE SCHOOL FOR SCANDAL

BY R. B. SHERIDAN, ESQ.

Tell me, ye prim adepts in Scandal's school,
Who rail by precept, and detract by rule,
Lives there no character, so tried, so known,
So decked with grace, and so unlike your own,
That even you assist her fame to raise,   5
Approve by envy, and by silence praise!
Attend! — a model shall attract your view —
Daughters of calumny, I summon you!
You shall decide if this a portrait prove,
Or fond creation of the Muse and Love.   10
Attend, ye virgin critics, shrewd and sage,
Ye matron censors of this childish age,
Whose peering eye and wrinkled front declare
A fixed antipathy to young and fair;
By cunning, cautious; or by nature, cold,   15
In maiden madness, virulently bold! —
Attend, ye skilled to coin the precious tale,

Creating proof, where inuendos fail!
Whose practised memories, cruelly exact,
Omit no circumstance, except the fact! —
Attend, all ye who boast, — or old or young, —
5 The living libel of a slanderous tongue!
So shall my theme as far contrasted be,
As saints by fiends, or hymns by calumny.
Come, gentle Amoret° (for 'neath that name
In worthier verse is sung thy beauty's fame);
10 Come — for but thee who seeks the Muse? and while
Celestial blushes check thy conscious smile,
With timid grace, and hesitating eye,
The perfect model, which I boast, supply: —
Vain Muse! couldst thou the humblest sketch create
15 Of her, or slightest charm couldst imitate —
Could thy blest strain in kindred colours trace
The faintest wonder of her form and face —
Poets would study the immortal line,
And Reynolds° own his art subdued by thine;
20 That art, which well might added lustre give
To Nature's best, and Heaven's superlative:
On Granby's° cheek might bid new glories rise,
Or point a purer beam from Devon's° eyes!
Hard is the task to shape that beauty's praise,
25 Whose judgment scorns the homage flattery pays!
But praising Amoret we cannot err,

No tongue o'ervalues Heaven, or flatters her!
Yet she by Fate's perverseness — she alone
Would doubt our truth, nor deem such praise her own.
Adorning fashion, unadorned by dress,
Simple from taste, and not from carelessness;   5
Discreet in gesture, in deportment mild,
Not stiff with prudence, nor uncouthly wild:
No state has Amoret; no studied mien;
She frowns no goddess, and she moves no queen.
The softer charm that in her manner lies   10
Is framed to captivate, yet not surprise;
It justly suits the expression of her face, —
'Tis less than dignity, and more than grace!
On her pure cheek the native hue is such,
That, formed by Heaven to be admired so much,   15
The hand divine, with a less partial care,
Might well have fixed a fainter crimson there,
And bade the gentle inmate of her breast —
Inshrinèd Modesty — supply the rest.
But who the peril of her lips shall paint?   20
Strip them of smiles — still, still all words are faint.
But moving Love himself appears to teach
Their action, though denied to rule her speech;
And thou who seest her speak, and dost not hear,
Mourn not her distant accents 'scape thine ear;   25
Viewing those lips, thou still may'st make pretence

To judge of what she says, and swear 'tis sense:
Clothed with such grace, with such expression fraught,
They move in meaning, and they pause in thought!
But dost thou farther watch, with charmed surprise,
5 The mild irresolution of her eyes,
Curious to mark how frequent they repose,
In brief eclipse and momentary close —
Ah! seest thou not an ambushed Cupid there,
Too timorous of his charge, with jealous care
10 Veils and unveils those beams of heavenly light,
Too full, too fatal else, for mortal sight?
Nor yet, such pleasing vengeance fond to meet,
In pardoning dimples hope a safe retreat.
What though her peaceful breast should ne'er allow
15 Subduing frowns to arm her altered brow,
By Love, I swear, and by his gentle wiles,
More fatal still the mercy of her smiles!
Thus lovely, thus adorned, possessing all
Of bright or fair that can to woman fall,
20 The height of vanity might well be thought
Prerogative in her, and Nature's fault.
Yet gentle Amoret, in mind supreme
As well as charms, rejects the vainer theme;
And, half mistrustful of her beauty's store,
25 She barbs with wit those darts too keen before: —
Read in all knowledge that her sex should reach,

Though Greville,° or the Muse, should deign to teach,
Fond to improve, nor timorous to discern
How far it is a woman's grace to learn;
In Millar's° dialect she would not prove
Apollo's priestess, but Apollo's love,   5
Graced by those signs which truth delights to own,
The timid blush, and mild submitted tone:
Whate'er she says, though sense appear throughout,
Displays the tender hue of female doubt;
Decked with that charm, how lovely wit appears,   10
How graceful science, when that robe she wears!
Such too her talents, and her bent of mind,
As speak a sprightly heart by thought refined:
A taste for mirth, by contemplation schooled,
A turn for ridicule, by candour ruled,   15
A scorn of folly, which she tries to hide;
An awe of talent, which she owns with pride!
     Peace, idle Muse! no more thy strain prolong,
But yield a theme, thy warmest praises wrong;
Just to her merit, though thou canst not raise   20
Thy feeble verse, behold th' acknowledged praise
Has spread conviction through the envious train,
And cast a fatal gloom o'er Scandal's reign!
And lo! each pallid hag, with blistered tongue,
Mutters assent to all thy zeal has sung —   25
Owns all the colours just — the outline true;
Thee my inspirer, and my model — CREWE!

PROLOGUE

WRITTEN BY MR. GARRICK°

    A School for Scandal! tell me, I beseech you,
Needs there a school this modish art to teach you?
No need of lessons now, the knowing think;
We might as well be taught to eat and drink.
5 Caused by a dearth of scandal, should the vapours°
Distress our fair ones — let them read the papers;
Their powerful mixtures such disorders hit;
Crave what you will — there's *quantum sufficit.*°
"Lord!" cries my Lady Wormwood (who loves
    tattle,
10 And puts much salt and pepper in her prattle),
Just risen at noon, all night at cards when threshing
Strong tea and scandal — "Bless me, how refresh-
    ing!
Give me the papers, Lisp — how bold and free! [*Sips.*
Last night Lord L. [*Sips*] *was caught with Lady D.*
15 For aching heads what charming sal volatile! [*Sips.*
If Mrs. B. will still continue flirting,
We hope she'll DRAW, *or we'll* UNDRAW *the curtain.*
Fine satire, poz° — in public all abuse it,
But, by ourselves [*Sips*], our praise we can't refuse it.

154

Now, Lisp, read you — there, at that dash and
   star:"
"Yes, ma'am — *A certain lord had best beware,*
Who lives not twenty miles from Grosvenor Square°;
For, should he Lady W. find willing,
Wormwood is bitter" —— "Oh! that's me! the
   villain! 5
Throw it behind the fire, and never more
Let that vile paper come within my door."
Thus at our friends we laugh, who feel the dart;
To reach our feelings, we ourselves must smart.
Is our young bard so young, to think that he 10
Can stop the full spring-tide of calumny?
Knows he the world so little, and its trade?
Alas! the devil's sooner raised than laid.
So strong, so swift, the monster there's no gagging:
Cut Scandal's head off, still the tongue is wagging. 15
Proud of your smiles once lavishly bestowed,
Again our young Don Quixote° takes the road:
To show his gratitude he draws his pen,
And seeks this hydra, Scandal, in his den.
For your applause all perils he would through — 20
He'll fight — that's write — a cavalliero true,
Till every drop of blood — that's ink — is spilt for
   you.

ACT I

SCENE I. *Lady Sneerwell's Dressing-room*

LADY SNEERWELL *discovered at her toilet;* SNAKE
drinking chocolate

Lady Sneer. The paragraphs, you say, Mr. Snake,°
were all inserted?

Snake. They were, madam; and, as I copied them
myself in a feigned hand, there can be no suspicion
5 whence they came.

Lady Sneer. Did you circulate the report of Lady
Brittle's intrigue with Captain Boastall?

Snake. That's in as fine a train as your ladyship
could wish. In the common course of things, I
10 think it must reach Mrs. Clackitt's ears within four-
and-twenty hours; and then, you know, the business
is as good as done.

Lady Sneer. Why, truly, Mrs. Clackitt has a very
pretty talent, and a great deal of industry.

15 *Snake.* True, madam, and has been tolerably successful in her day. To my knowledge, she has been
the cause of six matches being broken off, and three
sons being disinherited; of four forced elopements,
nine separate maintenances, and two divorces. Nay,

156

I have more than once traced her causing a *tête-à-
tête* in the "Town and Country Magazine,°" when the
parties, perhaps, had never seen each other's face
before in the course of their lives.

Lady Sneer. She certainly has talents, but her 5
manner is gross.

Snake. 'Tis very true. She generally designs well,
has a free tongue and a bold invention; but her
colouring is too dark, and her outlines often extravagant. She wants that delicacy of tint, and mel- 10
lowness of sneer, which distinguish your ladyship's
scandal.

Lady Sneer. You are partial, Snake.

Snake. Not in the least; every body allows that
Lady Sneerwell can do more with a word or look than 15
many can with the most laboured detail, even when
they happen to have a little truth on their side to
support it.

Lady Sneer. Yes, my dear Snake; and I am no
hypocrite to deny the satisfaction I reap from the 20
success of my efforts. Wounded myself, in the early
part of my life, by the envenomed tongue of slander,
I confess I have since known no pleasure equal to
the reducing others to the level of my own reputation.   25

Snake. Nothing can be more natural. But, Lady

Sneerwell, there is one affair in which you have
lately employed me, wherein, I confess, I am at a
loss to guess your motives.

Lady Sneer. I conceive you mean with respect to
5 my neighbour, Sir Peter Teazle, and his family?

Snake. I do.   Here are two young men, to whom
Sir Peter has acted as a kind of guardian since their
father's death;   the eldest possessing the most
amiable character, and universally well spoken of —
10 the youngest, the most dissipated and extravagant
young fellow in the kingdom, without friends or
character: the former an avowed admirer of your
ladyship, and apparently your favourite; the latter
attached to Maria, Sir Peter's ward, and confessedly
15 beloved by her. Now, on the face of these circumstances, it is utterly unaccountable to me, why
you, the widow of a city knight, with a good jointure,
should not close with° the passion of a man of such
character and expectations as Mr. Surface; and more
20 so why you should be so uncommonly earnest to
destroy the mutual attachment subsisting between
his brother Charles and Maria.

Lady Sneer. Then, at once to unravel this mystery,
I must inform you that love has no share whatever
25 in the intercourse between Mr. Surface and me.

Snake. No!

Lady Sneer. His real attachment is to Maria, or
her fortune; but, finding in his brother a favoured
rival, he has been obliged to mask his pretensions,
and profit by my assistance.

Snake. Yet still I am more puzzled why you should 5
interest yourself in his success.

Lady Sneer. Heavens! how dull you are! Cannot you surmise the weakness which I hitherto,
through shame, have concealed even from you?
Must I confess that Charles — that extravagant, 10
that bankrupt in fortune and reputation — that he
it is for whom I am thus anxious and malicious, and
to gain whom I would sacrifice every thing?

Snake. Now, indeed, your conduct appears con-
sistent: but how came you and Mr. Surface so con- 15
fidential?

Lady Sneer. For our mutual interest. I have
found him out a long time since. I know him to be
artful, selfish, and malicious — in short, a sentimental knave; while with Sir Peter, and indeed with 20
all his acquaintance, he passes for a youthful miracle
of prudence, good sense, and benevolence.

Snake. Yes; yet Sir Peter vows he has not his
equal in England; and, above all, he praises him as a
man of sentiment.   25

Lady Sneer. True; and with the assistance of his

sentiment and hypocrisy he has brought Sir Peter
entirely into his interest with regard to Maria; while
poor Charles has no friend in the house — though, I
fear, he has a powerful one in Maria's heart, against
5 whom we must direct our schemes.

Enter SERVANT

Ser. Mr. Surface.
Lady Sneer. Show him up. [*Exit* SERVANT.]
He generally calls about this time. I don't wonder
at people giving him to me for a lover.

Enter JOSEPH SURFACE

10   *Jos. Surf.* My dear Lady Sneerwell, how do you
do to-day? Mr. Snake, your most obedient.
Lady Sneer. Snake has just been rallying me on
our mutual attachment, but I have informed him of
our real views. You know how useful he has been
15 to us; and, believe me, the confidence is not ill-
placed.
Jos. Surf. Madam, it is impossible for me to suspect a man of Mr. Snake's sensibility and discernment.
Lady Sneer. Well, well, no compliments now;
20 but tell me when you saw your mistress, Maria — or,
what is more material to me, your brother.

Jos. Surf. I have not seen either since I left you; but I can inform you that they never meet. Some of your stories have taken a good effect, on Maria.

Lady Sneer. Ah, my dear Snake! the merit of this belongs to you. But do your brother's dis- 5 tresses increase?

Jos. Surf. Every hour. I am told he has had another execution° in the house yesterday. In short, his dissipation and extravagance exceed any thing I have ever heard of.   10

Lady Sneer. Poor Charles!

Jos. Surf. True, madam; notwithstanding his vices, one can't help feeling for him. Poor Charles! I'm sure I wish it were in my power to be of any essential service to him; for the man who does 15 not share in the distresses of a brother, even though merited by his own misconduct, deserves ——

Lady Sneer. O Lud°! you are going to be moral, and forget that you are among friends.

Jos. Surf. Egad,° that's true! I'll keep that 20 sentiment till I see Sir Peter. However, it is certainly a charity to rescue Maria from such a libertine, who if he is to be reclaimed, can be so only by a person of your ladyship's superior accomplishments and understanding.   25

Snake. I believe, Lady Sneerwell, here's company

M

coming: I'll go and copy the letter I mentioned to you. Mr. Surface, your most obedient.

Jos. Surf. Sir, your very devoted. — [*Exit* SNAKE.] Lady Sneerwell, I am very sorry you 5 have put any farther confidence in that fellow.

Lady Sneer. Why so?

Jos. Surf. I have lately detected him in frequent conference with old Rowley, who was formerly my father's steward, and has never, you know, been 10 a friend of mine.

Lady Sneer. And do you think he would betray us?

Jos. Surf. Nothing more likely: take my word for't, Lady Sneerwell, that fellow hasn't virtue 15 enough to be faithful even to his own villany. Ah, Maria!

Enter MARIA

Lady Sneer. Maria, my dear, how do you do? What's the matter?

Mar. Oh! there's that disagreeable lover of 20 mine, Sir Benjamin Backbite, has just called at my guardian's, with his odious uncle, Crabtree; so I slipped out, and ran hither to avoid them.

Lady Sneer. Is that all?

Jos. Surf. If my brother Charles had been of the party, madam, perhaps you would not have been so much alarmed.

Lady Sneer. Nay, now you are severe; for I dare swear the truth of the matter is, Maria heard 5 you were here. But, my dear, what has Sir Benjamin done, that you should avoid him so?

Mar. Oh, he has done nothing — but 'tis for what he has said: his conversation is a perpetual libel on all his acquaintance.   10

Jos. Surf. Ay, and the worst of it is, there is no advantage in not knowing him; for he'll abuse a stranger just as soon as his best friend: and his uncle's as bad.

Lady Sneer. Nay, but we should make allowance; 15 Sir Benjamin is a wit and a poet.

Mar. For my part, I own, madam, wit loses its respect with me, when I see it in company with malice. What do you think, Mr. Surface?

Jos. Surf. Certainly, madam; to smile at the 20 jest which plants a thorn in another's breast is to become a principal in the mischief.

Lady Sneer. Pshaw! there's no possibility of being witty without a little ill nature: the malice of a good thing is the barb that makes it stick. What's 25 your opinion, Mr. Surface?

Jos. Surf. To be sure, madam; that conversation, where the spirit of raillery is suppressed, will ever appear tedious and insipid.

Mar. Well, I'll not debate how far scandal may
5 be allowable; but in a man, I am sure, it is always contemptible. We have pride, envy, rivalship, and a thousand motives to depreciate each other; but the male slanderer must have the cowardice of a woman before he can traduce one.

Reënter SERVANT

10   *Ser.* Madam, Mrs. Candour is below, and, if your ladyship's at leisure, will leave her carriage.

Lady Sneer. Beg her to walk in. — [*Exit* SERVANT.] Now, Maria, here is a character to your taste; for, though Mrs. Candour is a little talkative,
15 every body allows her to be the best natured and best sort of woman.

Mar. Yes, with a very gross affectation of good nature and benevolence, she does more mischief than the direct malice of old Crabtree.

20   *Jos. Surf.* I' faith that's true, Lady Sneerwell: whenever I hear the current running against the characters of my friends, I never think them in such danger as when Candour undertakes their defence.

Lady Sneer. Hush! — here she is!

Enter Mrs. Candour

Mrs. Can. My dear Lady Sneerwell, how have you been this century? — Mr. Surface, what news do you hear? — though indeed it is no matter, for I think one hears nothing else but scandal.   5

Jos. Surf. Just so, indeed, ma'am.

Mrs. Can. Oh, Maria! child, — what, is the whole affair off between you and Charles? His extravagance, I presume — the town talks of nothing else.   10

Mar. I am very sorry, ma'am, the town has so little to do.

Mrs. Can. True, true, child: but there's no stopping people's tongues. I own I was hurt to hear it, as I indeed was to learn, from the same 15 quarter, that your guardian, Sir Peter, and Lady Teazle have not agreed lately as well as could be wished.

Mar. 'Tis strangely impertinent for people to busy themselves so.   20

Mrs. Can. Very true, child: but what's to be done? People will talk — there's no preventing it. Why, it was but yesterday I was told that Miss

Gadabout had eloped with Sir Filigree Flirt. But, Lord! there's no minding what one hears; though, to be sure, I had this from very good authority.

Mar. Such reports are highly scandalous.

5 *Mrs. Can.* So they are, child — shameful, shameful! But the world is so censorious, no character escapes. Lord, now who would have suspected your friend, Miss Prim, of an indiscretion? Yet such is the ill nature of people, that they say her 10 uncle stopped her last week, just as she was stepping into the York Mail° with her dancing-master.

Mar. I'll answer for't there are no grounds for that report.

Mrs. Can. Ah, no foundation in the world, I dare 15 swear; no more, probably, than for the story circulated last month, of Mrs. Festino's affair with Colonel Cassino — though, to be sure, that matter was never rightly cleared up.

Jos. Surf. The licence of invention some people 20 take is monstrous indeed.

Mar. 'Tis so; but, in my opinion, those who report such things are equally culpable.

Mrs. Can. To be sure they are; tale-bearers are as bad as the tale-makers — 'tis an old observa-25 tion, and a very true one: but what's to be done, as I said before? how will you prevent people

from talking? To-day, Mrs. Clackitt assured me,
Mr. and Mrs. Honeymoon were at last become
mere man and wife, like the rest of their acquaintance. And at the same time Miss Tattle, who was
by, affirmed, that Lord Buffalo had discovered 5
his lady at a house of no extraordinary fame; and
that Sir Harry Bouquet and Tom Saunter were to
measure swords on a similar provocation. But,
Lord, do you think I would report these things!
No, no! tale-bearers, as I said before, are just 10
as bad as the tale-makers.

Jos. Surf. Ah! Mrs. Candour, if every body had
your forbearance and good nature!

Mrs. Can. I confess, Mr. Surface, I cannot bear
to hear people attacked behind their backs; and 15
when ugly circumstances come out against our
acquaintance, I own I always love to think the
best. By the by, I hope 'tis not true that your
brother is absolutely ruined?

Jos. Surf. I am afraid his circumstances are very 20
bad indeed, ma'am.

Mrs. Can. Ah! I heard so — but you must tell
him to keep up his spirits; every body almost
is in the same way: Lord Spindle, Sir Thomas
Splint, Captain Quinze, and Mr. Nickit — all up, 25
I hear, within this week; so, if Charles is undone,

he'll find half his acquaintance ruined too, and
that, you know, is a consolation.

Jos. Surf. Doubtless, ma'am — a very great one.

Reënter SERVANT

Ser. Mr. Crabtree and Sir Benjamin Backbite.

[*Exit.*

5 *Lady Sneer.* So, Maria, you see your lover pur-
sues you; positively you sha'n't escape.

Enter CRABTREE *and* SIR BENJAMIN BACKBITE

Crab. Lady Sneerwell, I kiss your hand. Mrs.
Candour, I don't believe you are acquainted with
my nephew, Sir Benjamin Backbite? Egad,
10 ma'am, he has a pretty wit, and is a pretty poet
too. Isn't he, Lady Sneerwell?

Sir Ben. Oh, fie, uncle!

Crab. Nay, egad it's true; I back him at a rebus°
or a charade against the best rhymer in the king-
15 dom. Has your ladyship heard the epigram he
wrote last week on Lady Frizzle's feather catching
fire? — Do, Benjamin, repeat it, or the charade
you made last night extempore at Mrs. Drowzie's
conversazione.° Come now; your first is the
20 name of a fish, your second a great naval commander, and ——

Sir Ben. Uncle, now — pr'ythee ——

Crab. I' faith, ma'am, 'twould surprise you to hear how ready he is at all these sort of things.

Lady Sneer. I wonder, Sir Benjamin, you never publish any thing.   5

Sir Ben. To say truth, ma'am, 'tis very vulgar to print; and as my little productions are mostly satires and lampoons on particular people, I find they circulate more by giving copies in confidence to the friends of the parties.   However, I have 10 some love elegies, which, when favoured with this lady's smiles, I mean to give the public.

[*Pointing to* MARIA.

Crab. [*To* MARIA.] 'Fore heaven, ma'am, they'll immortalize you! — you will be handed down to posterity, like Petrarch's Laura,° or Waller's 15 Sacharissa.°

Sir Ben. [*To* MARIA.] Yes, madam, I think you will like them, when you shall see them on a beauti- ful quarto page, where a neat rivulet of text shall meander through a meadow of margin.   'Fore Gad 20 they will be the most elegant things of their kind!

Crab. But, ladies, that's true — have you heard the news?

Mrs. Can. What, sir, do you mean the report of ——   25

Crab. No, ma'am, that's not it. — Miss Nicely
is going to be married to her own footman.

Mrs. Can. Impossible!

Crab. Ask Sir Benjamin.

5   *Sir Ben.* 'Tis very true, ma'am: every thing is
fixed, and the wedding liveries bespoke.

Crab. Yes — and they do say there were pressing
reasons for it.

Lady Sneer. Why, I have heard something of
10 this before.

Mrs. Can. It can't be — and I wonder any one
should believe such a story of so prudent a lady
as Miss Nicely.

Sir Ben. O Lud! ma'am, that's the very reason
15 'twas believed at once. She has always been so
cautious and so reserved, that every body was sure
there was some reason for it at bottom.

Mrs. Can. Why, to be sure, a tale of scandal is
as fatal to the credit of a prudent lady of her stamp
20 as a fever is generally to those of the strongest
constitutions. But there is a sort of puny sickly
reputation, that is always ailing, yet will outlive
the robuster characters of a hundred prudes.

Sir Ben. True, madam, there are valetudina-
25 rians in reputation as well as constitution, who,
being conscious of their weak part, avoid the least

breath of air, and supply their want of stamina by
care and circumspection.

Mrs. Can. Well, but this may be all a mistake.
You know, Sir Benjamin, very trifling circumstances often give rise to the most injurious tales. 5

Crab. That they do, I'll be sworn, ma'am.   O
Lud! Mr. Surface, pray is it true that your uncle,
Sir Oliver, is coming home?

Jos. Surf. Not that I know of, indeed, sir.

Crab. He has been in the East Indies a long 10
time. You can scarcely remember him, I believe?
Sad comfort, whenever he returns, to hear how
your brother has gone on!

Jos. Surf. Charles has been imprudent, sir, to be
sure; but I hope no busy people have already 15
prejudiced Sir Oliver against him. He may
reform.

Sir Ben. To be sure he may: for my part, I
never believed him to be so utterly void of principle
as people say; and, though he has lost all his 20
friends, I am told nobody is better spoken of by
the Jews.

Crab. That's true, egad, nephew. If the Old
Jewry° was a ward, I believe Charles would be
an alderman: no man more popular there, 'fore 25
Gad! I hear he pays as many annuities as the

Irish tontine°; and that, whenever he is sick, they have prayers for the recovery of his health in all the synagogues.

Sir Ben. Yet no man lives in greater splendour.
5 They tell me, when he entertains his friends he will sit down to dinner with a dozen of his own securities; have a score of tradesmen waiting in the antechamber, and an officer behind every guest's chair.

10   *Jos. Surf.* This may be entertainment to you, gentlemen, but you pay very little regard to the feelings of a brother.

Mar. [*Aside.*] Their malice is intolerable! — [*Aloud.*] Lady Sneerwell, I must wish you a good
15 morning: I'm not very well.   [*Exit.*

Mrs. Can. O dear! she changes colour very much.

Lady Sneer. Do, Mrs. Candour, follow her: she may want your assistance.

20   *Mrs. Can.* That I will, with all my soul, ma'am. — Poor dear girl, who knows what her situation may be!   [*Exit.*

Lady Sneer. 'Twas nothing but that she could not bear to hear Charles reflected on, notwith-
25 standing their difference.

Sir Ben. The young lady's *penchant*° is obvious.

Crab. But, Benjamin, you must not give up the pursuit for that: follow her, and put her into good humour. Repeat her some of your own verses. Come, I'll assist you.

Sir Ben. Mr. Surface, I did not mean to hurt 5 you; but depend on't your brother is utterly undone.

Crab. O Lud, ay! undone as ever man was — can't raise a guinea!

Sir Ben. And every thing sold, I'm told, that 10 was movable.

Crab. I have seen one that was at his house. Not a thing left but some empty bottles that were overlooked, and the family pictures, which I believe are framed in the wainscots.   15

Sir Ben. And I'm very sorry also to hear some bad stories against him.   [*Going.*

Crab. Oh, he has done many mean things, that's certain.

Sir Ben. But, however, as he's your brother —— 20
                                         [*Going.*

Crab. We'll tell you all another opportunity.

Exeunt CRABTREE *and* SIR BENJAMIN

Lady Sneer. Ha! ha! 'tis very hard for them to leave a subject they have not quite run down.

Jos. Surf. And I believe the abuse was no more acceptable to your ladyship than Maria.

Lady Sneer. I doubt her affections are farther engaged than we imagine. But the family are ₅ to be here this evening, so you may as well dine where you are, and we shall have an opportunity of observing farther; in the meantime, I'll go and plot mischief, and you shall study sentiment.

[*Exeunt.*

SCENE II. *A Room in Sir Peter Teazle's House*

Enter SIR PETER TEAZLE

Sir Pet. When an old bachelor marries a young ₁₀ wife, what is he to expect? 'Tis now six months since Lady Teazle made me the happiest of men — and I have been the most miserable dog ever since! We tiffed a little going to church, and fairly quarrelled before the bells had done ringing. ₁₅ I was more than once nearly choked with gall during the honeymoon, and had lost all comfort in life before my friends had done wishing me joy. Yet I chose with caution — a girl bred wholly in the country, who never knew luxury beyond one ₂₀ silk gown, nor dissipation above the annual gala

of a race ball. Yet she now plays her part in
all the extravagant fopperies of fashion and the
town, with as ready a grace as if she never had
seen a bush or a grass-plot out of Grosvenor Square!
I am sneered at by all my acquaintance, and par- 5
agraphed in the newspapers. She dissipates my
fortune, and contradicts all my humours; yet
the worst of it is, I doubt I love her, or I should
never bear all this. However, I'll never be weak
enough to own it.   10

Enter ROWLEY

Row. Oh! Sir Peter, your servant: how is it
with you, sir?
Sir Pet. Very bad, Master Rowley, very bad.
I meet with nothing but crosses and vexations.
Row. What can have happened since yesterday? 15
Sir Pet. A good question to a married man!
Row. Nay, I'm sure, Sir Peter, your lady can't
be the cause of your uneasiness.
Sir Pet. Why, has any body told you she was
dead?   20
Row. Come, come, Sir Peter, you love her,
notwithstanding your tempers don't exactly agree.
Sir Pet. But the fault is entirely hers, Master

Rowley. I am, myself, the sweetest-tempered man
alive, and hate a teasing temper; and so I tell
her a hundred times a day.

    Row. Indeed!

5   *Sir Pet.* Ay; and what is very extraordinary,
in all our disputes she is always in the wrong!
But Lady Sneerwell, and the set she meets at her
house, encourage the perverseness of her disposition. Then, to complete my vexation, Maria,
10 my ward, whom I ought to have the power of
a father over, is determined to turn rebel too,
and absolutely refuses the man whom I have long
resolved on for her husband; meaning, I suppose,
to bestow herself on his profligate brother.

15   *Row.* You know, Sir Peter, I have always taken
the liberty to differ with you on the subject of
these two young gentlemen. I only wish you
may not be deceived in your opinion of the elder.
For Charles, my life on't! he will retrieve his errors
20 yet. Their worthy father, once my honoured master, was, at his years, nearly as wild a spark; yet,
when he died, he did not leave a more benevolent
heart to lament his loss.

    Sir Pet. You are wrong, Master Rowley. On
25 their father's death, you know, I acted as a kind
of guardian to them both, till their uncle Sir Oliver's

liberality gave them an early independence: of
course, no person could have more opportunities
of judging of their hearts, and I was never mistaken in my life.   Joseph is indeed a model for
the young men of the age.   He is a man of senti- 5
ment, and acts up to the sentiments he professes;
but, for the other, take my word for't, if he had
any grain of virtue by descent, he has dissipated
it with the rest of his inheritance.   Ah! my old
friend, Sir Oliver, will be deeply mortified when he 10
finds how part of his bounty has been misapplied.

Row. I am sorry to find you so violent against
the young man, because this may be the most
critical period of his fortune.   I came hither with
news that will surprise you.   15

Sir Pet. What! let me hear.

Row. Sir Oliver is arrived, and at this moment
in town.

Sir Pet. How! you astonish me!   I thought you
did not expect him this month.   20

Row. I did not: but his passage has been remarkably quick.

Sir Pet. Egad, I shall rejoice to see my old friend.
'Tis sixteen years since we met.   We have had many
a day together: — but does he still enjoin us not 25
to inform his nephews of his arrival?

N

Row. Most strictly. He means, before it is
known, to make some trial of their dispositions.

Sir Pet. Ah! there needs no art to discover
their merits — however, he shall have his way;
5 but, pray, does he know I am married?

Row. Yes, and will soon wish you joy.

Sir Pet. What, as we drink health to a friend
in a consumption! Ah! Oliver will laugh at me.
We used to rail at matrimony together, but he
10 has been steady to his text. Well, he must be
soon at my house, though — I'll instantly give
orders for his reception. But, Master Rowley,
don't drop a word that Lady Teazle and I ever
disagree.

15 *Row.* By no means.

Sir Pet. For I should never be able to stand
Noll's jokes; so I'll have him think, Lord forgive
me! that we are a very happy couple.

Row. I understand you: — but then you must
20 be very careful not to differ while he is in the house
with you.

Sir Pet. Egad, and so we must — and that's
impossible. Ah! Master Rowley, when an old
bachelor marries a young wife, he deserves — no
25 — the crime carries its punishment along with
it.   [*Exeunt.*

ACT II

SCENE I. *A room in Sir Peter Teazle's House*

Enter SIR PETER *and* LADY TEAZLE

Sir Pet. Lady Teazle, Lady Teazle, I'll not bear it!

Lady Teaz. Sir Peter, Sir Peter, you may bear it or not, as you please; but I ought to have my own way in every thing, and, what's more, I will 5 too. What! though I was educated in the country, I know very well that women of fashion in London are accountable to nobody after they are married.

Sir Pet. Very well, ma'am, very well; so a husband is to have no influence, no authority? 10

Lady Teaz. Authority! No, to be sure: if you wanted authority over me, you should have adopted me, and not married me: I am sure you were old enough.

Sir Pet. Old enough! — ay, there it is. Well, 15 well, Lady Teazle, though my life may be made unhappy by your temper, I'll not be ruined by your extravagance!

179

Lady Teaz. My extravagance! I'm sure I'm
not more extravagant than a woman of fashion
ought to be.

Sir Pet. No, no, madam, you shall throw away
5 no more sums on such unmeaning luxury.   'Slife°!
to spend as much to furnish your dressing-room
with flowers in winter as would suffice to turn the
Pantheon° into a greenhouse, and give a *fête champêtre*° at Christmas.

10   *Lady Teaz.* And am I to blame, Sir Peter, because flowers are dear in cold weather?   You should
find fault with the climate, and not with me.   For
my part, I'm sure I wish it was spring all the year
round, and that roses grew under our feet!

15   *Sir Pet.* Oons°!   madam — if you had been
born to this, I shouldn't wonder at you talking
thus ; but you forget what your situation was
when I married you.

Lady Teaz. No, no, I don't; 'twas a very dis-
20 agreeable one, or I should never have married you.

Sir Pet. Yes, yes, madam, you were then in
somewhat a humbler style — the daughter of a
plain   country   squire.   Recollect, Lady Teazle,
when I saw you first sitting at your tambour,
25 in a pretty figured linen gown, with a bunch of
keys at your side, your hair combed smooth over

a roll, and your apartment hung round with fruits
in worsted, of your own working.

Lady Teaz. Oh, yes! I remember it very well,
and a curious life I led. My daily occupation to
inspect the dairy, superintend the poultry, make 5
extracts from the family receipt-book, and comb
my aunt Deborah's lapdog.

Sir Pet. Yes, yes, ma'am, 'twas so indeed.

Lady Teaz. And then you know, my evening
amusements! To draw patterns for ruffles, which 10
I had not materials to make up; to play Pope
Joan° with the curate; to read a sermon to my
aunt; or to be stuck down to an old spinet to strum
my father to sleep after a fox-chase.

Sir Pet. I am glad you have so good a memory. 15
Yes, madam, these were the recreations I took
you from; but now you must have your coach
— *vis-à-vis*° — and three powdered footmen before
your chair°; and, in the summer, a pair of white
cats to draw you to Kensington Gardens.° No rec- 20
ollection, I suppose, when you were content to ride
double, behind the butler, on a docked coach-horse.

Lady Teaz. No — I swear I never did that: I
deny the butler and the coach-horse.

Sir Pet. This, madam, was your situation; and 25
what have I done for you? I have made you a

woman of fashion, of fortune, of rank — in short,
I have made you my wife.

Lady Teaz. Well, then, and there is but one
thing more you can make me to add to the obliga-
5 tion, that is ——

Sir Pet. My widow, I suppose?

Lady Teaz. Hem! hem!

Sir Pet. I thank you, madam — but don't
flatter yourself, for, though your ill conduct may
10 disturb my peace of mind, it shall never break my
heart, I promise you: however, I am equally obliged
to you for the hint.

Lady Teaz. Then why will you endeavour to
make yourself so disagreeable to me, and thwart
15 me in every little elegant expense?

Sir Pet. 'Slife, madam, I say, had you any of
these little elegant expenses when you married me?

Lady Teaz. Lud, Sir Peter! would you have me
be out of the fashion?

20   *Sir Pet.* The fashion, indeed! what had you to
do with the fashion before you married me?

Lady Teaz. For my part, I should think you
would like to have your wife thought a woman of
taste.

25   *Sir Pet.* Ay — there again — taste! Zounds!
madam, you had no taste when you married me!

Lady Teaz. That's very true, indeed, Sir Peter!

and, after having married you, I should never pretend to taste again, I allow. But now, Sir Peter,
since we have finished our daily jangle, I presume
I may go to my engagement at Lady Sneerwell's.

Sir Pet. Ay, there's another precious circumstance 5
— a charming set of acquaintance you have made
there!

Lady Teaz. Nay, Sir Peter, they are all people
of rank and fortune, and remarkably tenacious of
reputation.   10

Sir Pet. Yes, egad, they are tenacious of reputation with a vengeance; for they don't choose
any body should have a character but themselves!
Such a crew! Ah! many a wretch has rid on a
hurdle° who has done less mischief than these 15
utterers of forged tales, coiners of scandal, and
clippers of reputation.°

Lady Teaz. What, would you restrain the free-
dom of speech?

Sir Pet. Ah! they have made you just as bad 20
as any one of the society.

Lady Teaz. Why, I believe I do bear a part with
a tolerable grace.

Sir Pet. Grace indeed!

Lady Teaz. But I vow I bear no malice against 25
the people I abuse: when I say an ill-natured

thing, 'tis out of pure good humour; and I take it for granted they deal exactly in the same manner with me.   But, Sir Peter, you know you promised to come to Lady Sneerwell's too.

5   *Sir Pet.* Well, well, I'll call in, just to look after my own character.

Lady Teaz. Then, indeed, you must make haste after me, or you'll be too late.   So good-bye to ye.

[*Exit.*

Sir Pet. So — I have gained much by my in-
10 tended expostulation!   Yet with what a charming air she contradicts every thing I say, and how pleasantly she shows her contempt for my authority!   Well, though I can't make her love me, there is great satisfaction in quarrelling with her; and I
15 think she never appears to such advantage as when she is doing every thing in her power to plague me.   [*Exit.*

SCENE II.   *A Room in Lady Sneerwell's House.*

LADY   SNEERWELL,   MRS.   CANDOUR,   CRABTREE,
   SIR   BENJAMIN   BACKBITE,   *and*   JOSEPH   SURFACE,
   discovered

Lady Sneer. Nay, positively, we will hear it.
Jos. Surf. Yes, yes, the epigram, by all means.

Sir Ben. O plague on't, uncle! 'tis mere nonsense.

Crab. No, no; 'fore Gad, very clever for an extempore!

Sir Ben. But, ladies, you should be acquainted 5 with the circumstance. You must know, that one day last week, as Lady Betty Curricle was taking the dust in Hyde Park,° in a sort of duodecimo° phaeton, she desired me to write some verses on her ponies; upon which, I took out my 10 pocket-book, and in one moment produced the following:—.

Sure never were seen two such beautiful ponies;
Other horses are clowns, but these macaronies°:
To give them this title I'm sure can't be wrong, 15
Their legs are so slim, and their tails are so long.

Crab. There, ladies, done in the smack of a whip, and on horseback too.

Jos. Surf. A very Phœbus,° mounted — indeed, Sir Benjamin!   20

Sir Ben. Oh dear, sir! trifles — trifles.

Enter LADY TEAZLE *and* MARIA

Mrs. Can. I must have a copy.

Lady Sneer. Lady Teazle, I hope we shall see Sir Peter?

Lady Teaz. I believe he'll wait on your ladyship presently.

Lady Sneer. Maria, my love, you look grave. Come, you shall sit down to piquet° with Mr. Sur-
5 face.

Mar. I take very little pleasure in cards — however, I'll do as your ladyship pleases.

Lady Teaz. I am surprised Mr. Surface should sit down with her; I thought he would have em-
10 braced this opportunity of speaking to me before Sir Peter came.   [*Aside.*

Mrs. Can. Now, I'll die, but you are so scandalous, I'll forswear your society.

Lady Teaz. What's the matter, Mrs. Candour?
15 *Mrs. Can.* They'll not allow our friend Miss Vermilion to be handsome.

Lady Sneer. Oh, surely she is a pretty woman.

Crab. I am very glad you think so, ma'am.

Mrs. Can. She has a charming fresh colour.
20 *Lady Teaz.* Yes, when it is fresh put on.

Mrs. Can. Oh, fie! I'll swear her colour is natural: I have seen it come and go!

Lady Teaz. I dare swear you have, ma'am: it goes off at night, and comes again in the morn-
25 ing.

Sir Ben. True, ma'am, it not only comes and

goes; but, what's more, egad, her maid can fetch
and carry it!

Mrs. Can. Ha! ha! ha! how I hate to hear
you talk so! But surely, now, her sister is, or was,
very handsome.   5

Crab. Who? Mrs. Evergreen? O Lord! she's
six-and-fifty if she's an hour!

Mrs. Can. Now positively you wrong her;
fifty-two or fifty-three is the utmost — and I don't
think she looks more.   10

Sir Ben. Ah! there's no judging by her looks,
unless one could see her face.

Lady Sneer. Well, well, if Mrs. Evergreen does
take some pains to repair the ravages of time, you
must allow she effects it with great ingenuity; and 15
surely that's better than the careless manner in
which the widow Ochre caulks her wrinkles.

Sir Ben. Nay, now, Lady Sneerwell, you are
severe upon the widow. Come, come, 'tis not
that she paints so ill — but, when she has finished 20
her face, she joins it on so badly to her neck, that
she looks like a mended statue, in which the con-
noisseur may see at once that the head is modern,
though the trunk's antique.

Crab. Ha! ha! ha! Well said, nephew!   25

Mrs. Can. Ha! ha! ha! Well, you make me

laugh; but I vow I hate you for it. What do you
think of Miss Simper?

Sir Ben. Why, she has very pretty teeth.

Lady Teaz. Yes; and on that account, when
5 she is neither speaking nor laughing (which very
seldom happens), she never absolutely shuts her
mouth, but leaves it always a-jar, as it were —
thus.   [*Shows her teeth.*

Mrs. Can. How can you be so ill-natured?

10 *Lady Teaz.* Nay, I allow even that's better than
the pains Mrs. Prim takes to conceal her losses in
· front. She draws her mouth till it positively
resembles the aperture of a poor's-box,° and all her
words appear to slide out edgewise, as it were —
15 thus: *How do you do, madam? Yes, madam.*

[*Mimics.*

Lady Sneer. Very well, Lady Teazle; I see you
can be a little severe.

Lady Teaz. In defence of a friend it is but
justice. But here comes Sir Peter to spoil our
20 pleasantry.

Enter SIR PETER TEAZLE

Sir Pet. Ladies, your most obedient. — [*Aside.*]
Mercy on me, here is the whole set! a character
dead at every word, I suppose.

Mrs. Can. I am rejoiced you are come, Sir
Peter. They have been so censorious — and Lady
Teazle as bad as any one.

Sir Pet. That must be very distressing to you,
indeed, Mrs. Candour.   5

Mrs. Can. Oh, they will allow good qualities
to nobody; not even good nature to our friend
Mrs. Pursy.

Lady Teaz. What, the fat dowager who was at
Mrs. Quadrille's last night?   10

Mrs. Can. Nay, her bulk is her misfortune;
and, when she takes so much pains to get rid of it,
you ought not to reflect on her.

Lady Sneer. That's very true, indeed.

Lady Teaz. Yes, I know she almost lives on acids 15
and small whey; laces herself by pulleys; and
often, in the hottest noon in summer, you may
see her on a little squat pony, with her hair plaited
up behind like a drummer's and puffing round the
Ring° on a full trot.   20

Mrs. Can. I thank you, Lady Teazle, for defending her.

Sir Pet. Yes, a good defence, truly.

Mrs. Can. Truly, Lady Teazle is as censorious
as Miss Sallow.   25

Crab. Yes, and she is a curious being to pretend

to be censorious — an awkward gawky, without any one good point under heaven.

Mrs. Can. Positively you shall not be so very severe. Miss Sallow is a near relation of mine
5 by marriage, and, as for her person, great allowance is to be made; for, let me tell you, a woman labours under many disadvantages who tries to pass for a girl of six-and-thirty.

Lady Sneer. Though, surely, she is handsome
10 still — and for the weakness in her eyes, considering how much she reads by candlelight, it is not to be wondered at.

Mrs. Can. True, and then as to her manner; upon my word I think it is particularly graceful,
15 considering she never had the least education: for you know her mother was a Welsh milliner, and her father a sugar-baker at Bristol.

Sir Ben. Ah! you are both of you too good-natured!

20 *Sir Pet.* Yes, damned good-natured! This their own relation! mercy on me!   [*Aside.*

Mrs. Can. For my part, I own I cannot bear to hear a friend ill-spoken of.

Sir Pet. No, to be sure!

25 *Sir Ben.* Oh! you are of a moral turn. Mrs. Candour and I can sit for an hour and hear Lady Stucco talk sentiment.

Lady Teaz. Nay, I vow Lady Stucco is very well with the dessert after dinner; for she's just like the French fruit one cracks for mottoes — made up of paint and proverb.

Mrs. Can. Well, I will never join in ridiculing 5 a friend; and so I constantly tell my cousin Ogle, and you all know what pretensions she has to be critical on beauty.

Crab. Oh, to be sure! she has herself the oddest countenance that ever was seen; 'tis a collection 10 of features from all the different countries of the globe.

Sir Ben. So she has, indeed — an Irish front ——

Crab. Caledonian locks ——

Sir .Ben. Dutch nose ——   15

Crab. Austrian lips ——

Sir Ben. Complexion of a Spaniard ——

Crab. And teeth *à la Chinoise* ——

Sir Ben. In short, her face resembles a *table d'hôte* at Spa° — where no two guests are of a 20 nation ——

Crab. Or a congress at the close of a general war — wherein all the members, even to her eyes, appear to have a different interest, and her nose and chin are the only parties likely to join 25 issue.

Mrs. Can. Ha! ha! ha!

Sir Pet. Mercy on my life! — a person they dine with twice a week!   [*Aside.*

Mrs. Can. Nay, but I vow you shall not carry the laugh off so — for give me leave to say, that
5 Mrs. Ogle ——

Sir Pet. Madam, madam, I beg your pardon — there's no stopping these good gentlemen's tongues. But when I tell you, Mrs. Candour, that the lady they are abusing is a particular friend of mine,
10 I hope you'll not take her part.

Lady Sneer. Ha! ha! ha! well said, Sir Peter! but you are a cruel creature — too phlegmatic yourself for a jest, and too peevish to allow wit in others.

15 *Sir Pet.* Ah, madam, true wit is more nearly allied to good nature than your ladyship is aware of.

Lady Teaz. True, Sir Peter: I believe they are so near akin that they can never be united.

Sir Ben. Or rather, suppose them man and wife,
20 because one seldom sees them together.

Lady Teaz. But Sir Peter is such an enemy to scandal, I believe he would have it put down by parliament.

Sir Pet. 'Fore heaven, madam, if they were
25 to consider the sporting with reputation of as much importance as poaching on manors, and

pass an act for the preservation of fame, as well
as game, I believe many would thank them for
the bill.

Lady Sneer. O Lud! Sir Peter; would you de-
prive us of our privileges?   5

Sir Pet. Ay, madam; and then no person should
be permitted to kill characters and run down
reputations, but qualified old maids and disappointed widows.

Lady Sneer. Go, you monster!   10

Mrs. Can. But, surely, you would not be quite
so severe on .those who only report what they
hear?

Sir Pet. Yes, madam, I would have law mer-
chant° for them too; and in all cases of slander 15
currency, whenever the drawer of the lie was not
to be found, the injured parties should have a right
to come on any of the indorsers.°

Crab. Well, for my part, I believe there never
was a scandalous tale without some foundation. 2c

Lady Sneer. Come, ladies, shall we sit down to
cards in the next room?

Enter SERVANT, *who whispers* SIR PETER.

Sir Pet. I'll be with them directly. — [*Exit*
SERVANT.] I'll get away unperceived.   [*Aside.*
    o

Lady Sneer. Sir Peter, you are not going to leave us?

Sir Pet. Your ladyship must excuse me; I'm called away by particular business. But I leave
5 my character behind me.   [*Exit.*

Sir Ben. Well — certainly, Lady Teazle, that lord of yours is a strange being: I could tell you some stories of him would make you laugh heartily if he were not your husband.

10 *Lady Teaz.* Oh, pray don't mind that; come, do let's hear them.

[*Exeunt all but* JOSEPH SURFACE *and* MARIA.

Jos. Surf. Maria, I see you have no satisfaction in this society.

Mar. How is it possible I should? If to raise
15 malicious smiles at the infirmities or misfortunes of those who have never injured us be the province of wit or humour, Heaven grant me a double portion of dulness!

Jos. Surf. Yet they appear more ill-natured than
20 they are; they have no malice at heart.

Mar. Then is their conduct still more contemptible; for, in my opinion, nothing could excuse the intemperance of their tongues but a natural and uncontrollable bitterness of mind.

25 *Jos. Surf.* Undoubtedly, madam; and it has al-

ways been a sentiment of mine, that to propagate a
malicious truth wantonly is more despicable than to
falsify from revenge. But can you, Maria, feel thus
for others, and be unkind to me alone? Is hope to
be denied the tenderest passion?   5

Mar. Why will you distress me by renewing this
subject?

Jos. Surf. Ah, Maria! you would not treat me
thus, and oppose your guardian, Sir Peter's will,
but that I see that profligate Charles is still a favoured 10
rival.

Mar. Ungenerously urged! But, whatever my
sentiments are for that unfortunate young man, be
assured I shall not feel more bound to give him up,
because his distresses have lost him the regard even 15
of a brother.

Jos. Surf. Nay, but, Maria, do not leave me with a
frown: by all that's honest, I swear —— [*Kneels.*

Reënter LADY TEAZLE *behind*

[*Aside.*] Gad's life, here's Lady Teazle. — [*Aloud
to* MARIA.] You must not — no, you shall not — 20
for, though I have the greatest regard for Lady
Teazle ——

Mar. Lady Teazle!

Jos. Surf. Yet were Sir Peter to suspect ——

Lady Teaz. [*Coming forward.*] What is this, pray? Does he take her for me? — Child, you are wanted in the next room. — [*Exit* MARIA.] What is
5 all this, pray?

Jos. Surf. Oh, the most unlucky circumstance in nature! Maria has somehow suspected the tender concern I have for your happiness, and threatened to acquaint Sir Peter with her suspicions, and I was
10 just endeavouring to reason with her when you came in.

Lady Teaz. Indeed! but you seemed to adopt a very tender mode of reasoning — do you usually argue on your knees?

15 *Jos. Surf.* Oh, she's a child, and I thought a little bombast ——But, Lady Teazle, when are you to give me your judgment on my library, as you promised?

Lady Teaz. No, no; I begin to think it would be
20 imprudent, and you know I admit you as a lover no farther than fashion requires.

Jos. Surf. True — a mere Platonic cicisbeo,° what every wife is entitled to.

Lady Teaz. Certainly, one must not be out of
25 the fashion. However, I have so many of my country prejudices left, that, though Sir Peter's ill

humour may vex me ever so, it never shall provoke
me to——

Jos. Surf. The only revenge in your power.   Well,
I applaud your moderation.

Lady Teaz. Go — you are an insinuating wretch! 5
But we shall be missed — let us join the company.

Jos. Surf. But we had best not return together.

Lady Teaz. Well, don't stay; for Maria sha'n't
come to hear any more of your reasoning, I promise
you.   [*Exit.* 10

Jos. Surf. A curious dilemma, truly, my politics
have run me into!   I wanted, at first, only to in-
gratiate myself with Lady Teazle, that she might
not be my enemy with Maria; and I have, I don't
know how, become her serious lover.   Sincerely I 15
begin to wish I had never made such a point of gain-
ing so very good a character, for it has led me into
so many cursed rogueries that I doubt I shall be
exposed at last.   .   [*Exit.*

Scene III. *A Room in Sir Peter Teazle's House*

Enter Sir Oliver Surface *and* Rowley

Sir Oliv. Ha! ha! ha! so my old friend is married, hey? — a young wife out of the country. Ha! ha! ha! that he should have stood bluff to old bachelor so long, and sink into a husband at
5 last!

Row. But you must not rally him on the subject, Sir Oliver; 'tis a tender point, I assure you, though he has been married only seven months.

Sir Oliv. Then he has been just half a year on the
10 stool of repentance! — Poor Peter! But you say he has entirely given up Charles — never sees him, hey?

Row. His prejudice against him is astonishing, and I am sure greatly increased by a jealousy of
15 him with Lady Teazle, which he has industriously been led into by a scandalous society in the neighbourhood, who have contributed not a little to Charles's ill name. Whereas the truth is, I believe, if the lady is partial to either of them, his brother
20 is the favourite.

Sir Oliv. Ay, I know there are a set of malicious, prating, prudent gossips, both male and female,

who murder characters to kill time, and will rob a
young fellow of his good name before he has years
to know the value of it.   But I am not to be prejudiced against my nephew by such, I promise you!
No, no: if Charles has done nothing false or mean, I 5
shall compound° for his extravagance.

Row. Then, my life on't, you will reclaim him.
Ah, sir, it gives me new life to find that your heart
is not turned against him, and that the son of my
good old master has one friend, however, left.   10

Sir Oliv. What! shall I forget, Master Rowley,
when I was at his years myself?   Egad, my brother
and I were neither of us very prudent youths; and
yet, I believe, you have not seen many better men
than your old master was?   15

Row. Sir, 'tis this reflection gives me assurance
that Charles may yet be a credit to his family.   But
here comes Sir Peter.

Sir Oliv. Egad, so he does!   Mercy on me! he's
greatly altered, and seems to have a settled married 20
look!   One may read husband in his face at this
distance!

Enter SIR PETER TEAZLE

Sir Pet. Ha! Sir Oliver — my old friend! Welcome to England a thousand times!

Sir Oliv. Thank you, thank you, Sir Peter! and i' faith I am glad to find you well, believe me!

Sir Pet. Oh! 'tis a long time since we met — fifteen years, I doubt, Sir Oliver, and many a cross
5 accident in the time.

Sir Oliv. Ay, I have had my share. But, what! I find you are married, hey, my old boy? Well, well, it can't be helped; and so — I wish you joy with all my heart!

10 *Sir Pet.* Thank you, thank you, Sir Oliver. — Yes, I have entered into — the happy state; but we'll not talk of that now.

Sir Oliv. True, true, Sir Peter; old friends should not begin on grievances at first meeting. No, no,
15 no.

Row. [*Aside to* Sir Oliver.] Take care, pray, sir.

Sir Oliv. Well, so one of my nephews is a wild rogue, hey?

Sir Pet. Wild! Ah! my old friend, I grieve for
20 your disappointment there; he's a lost young man, indeed. However, his brother will make you amends; Joseph is, indeed, what a youth should be — every body in the world speaks well of him.

Sir Oliv. I am sorry to hear it; he has too good a
25 character to be an honest fellow. Every body speaks well of him! Pshaw! then he has bowed as

low to knaves and fools as to the honest dignity of
genius and virtue.

Sir Pet. What, Sir Oliver! do you blame him for
not making enemies?

Sir Oliv. Yes, if he has merit enough to deserve 5
them.

Sir Pet. Well, well — you'll be convinced when
you know him. 'Tis edification to hear him converse;
he professes the noblest sentiments.

Sir Oliv. Oh, plague of his sentiments! If he 10
salutes me with a scrap of morality in his mouth, I
shall be sick directly. But, however, don't mistake
me, Sir Peter; I don't mean to defend Charles's
errors: but, before I form my judgment of either of
them, I intend to make a trial of their hearts; and 15
my friend Rowley and I have planned something for
the purpose.

Row. And Sir Peter shall own for once he has been
mistaken.

Sir Pet. Oh, my life on Joseph's honour!   20

Sir Oliv. Well — come, give us a bottle of good
wine, and we'll drink the lads' health, and tell you
our scheme.

Sir Pet. *Allons*,° then!

Sir Oliv. And don't, Sir Peter, be so severe against 25
your old friend's son. Odds my life! I am not

sorry that he has run out of the course a little: for my part, I hate to see prudence clinging to the green suckers of youth; 'tis like ivy round a sapling, and spoils the growth of the tree.   [*Exeunt.*

ACT III

Scene I. *A Room in Sir Peter Teazle's House*

Enter Sir Peter Teazle, Sir Oliver Surface, *and* Rowley

Sir Pet. Well, then, we will see this fellow first, and have our wine afterwards. But how is this, Master Rowley? I don't see the jest of your scheme.

Row. Why, sir, this Mr. Stanley, whom I was 5 speaking of, is nearly related to them by their mother. He was once a merchant in Dublin, but has been ruined by a series of undeserved misfortunes. He has applied, by letter, since his confinement, both to Mr. Surface and Charles: from the 10 former he has received nothing but evasive promises of future service, while Charles has done all that his extravagance has left him power to do; and he is, at this time, endeavouring to raise a sum of money, part of which, in the midst of his own distresses, I 15 know he intends for the service of poor Stanley.

Sir Oliv. Ah! he is my brother's son.

Sir Pet. Well, but how is Sir Oliver personally to ——

Row. Why, sir, I will inform Charles and his brother that Stanley has obtained permission to apply personally to his friends; and, as they have neither of them ever seen him, let Sir Oliver assume 5 his character, and he will have a fair opportunity of judging, at least, of the benevolence of their dispositions: and believe me, sir, you will find in the youngest brother one who, in the midst of folly and dissipation, has still, as our immortal bard expresses 10 it, —

> "a heart to pity,° and a hand,
> Open as day, for melting charity."

Sir Pet. Pshaw! What signifies his having an open hand or purse either, when he has nothing left to 15 give? Well, well, make the trial, if you please. But where is the fellow whom you brought for Sir Oliver to examine, relative to Charles's affairs?

Row. Below, waiting his commands, and no one can give him better intelligence. — This, Sir Oliver, 20 is a friendly Jew, who, to do him justice, has done every thing in his power to bring your nephew to a proper sense of his extravagance.

Sir Pet. Pray let us have him in.

Row. Desire Mr. Moses to walk up stairs.

                                    [*Calls to* SERVANT.

Sir Pet. But, pray, why should you suppose he will speak the truth?

Row. Oh, I have convinced him that he has no chance of recovering certain sums advanced to Charles but through the bounty of Sir Oliver, 5 who he knows is arrived; so that you may depend on his fidelity to his own interests. I have also another evidence in my power, one Snake, whom I have detected in a matter little short of forgery, and shall shortly produce to remove some of your 10 prejudices, Sir Peter, relative to Charles and Lady Teazle.

Sir Pet. I have heard too much on that subject.

Row. Here comes the honest Israelite.

Enter MOSES

— This is Sir Oliver.   15

Sir Oliv. Sir, I understand you have lately had great dealings with my nephew Charles.

Mos. Yes, Sir Oliver, I have done all I could for him; but he was ruined before he came to me for assistance.   20

Sir Oliv. That was unlucky, truly; for you have had no opportunity of showing your talents.

Mos. None at all; I hadn't the pleasure of

knowing his distresses till he was some thousands worse than nothing.

Sir Oliv. Unfortunate, indeed! But I suppose you have done all in your power for him, honest
5 Moses?

Mos. Yes, he knows that. This very evening I was to have brought him a gentleman from the city, who does not know him, and will, I believe, advance him some money.

10 *Sir Pet.* What, one Charles has never had money from before?

Mos. Yes, Mr. Premium, of Crutched Friars,° formerly a broker.

Sir Pet. Egad, Sir Oliver, a thought strikes me! —
15 Charles, you say, does not know Mr. Premium?

Mos. Not at all.

Sir Pet. Now then, Sir Oliver, you may have a better opportunity of satisfying yourself than by an old romancing tale of a poor relation: go with my friend
20 Moses, and represent Premium, and then, I'll answer for it, you'll see your nephew in all his glory.

Sir Oliv. Egad, I like this idea better than the other, and I may visit Joseph afterwards as old Stanley.

25 *Sir Pet.* True — so you may.

Row. Well, this is taking Charles rather at a dis-

advantage, to be sure. However, Moses, you understand Sir Peter, and will be faithful?

Mos. You may depend upon me. — [*Looks
at his watch.*] This is near the time I was to have
gone.   5

Sir Oliv. I'll accompany you as soon as you please,
Moses —— But hold! I have forgot one thing —
how the plague shall I be able to pass for a Jew?

Mos. There's no need — the principal is Christian.

Sir Oliv. Is he? I'm very sorry to hear it. But, 10
then again, an't I rather too smartly dressed to
look like a money lender?

Sir Pet. Not at all; 'twoud not be out of character, if you went in your own carriage — would it,
Moses?   15

Mos. Not in the least.

Sir Oliv. Well, but how must I talk; there's
certainly some cant of usury and mode of treating
that I ought to know.

Sir Pet. Oh, there's not much to learn. The great 20
point, as I take it, is to be exorbitant enough in
your demands. Hey, Moses?

Mos. Yes, that's a very great point.

Sir Oliv. I'll answer for't I'll not be wanting in
that. I'll ask him eight or ten per cent. on the loan, 25
at least.

Mos. If you ask him no more than that, you'll
be discovered immediately.

Sir Oliv. Hey! what, the plague! how much
then?

5 *Mos.* That depends upon the circumstances. If
he appears not very anxious for the supply, you
should require only forty or fifty per cent.; but if
you find him in great distress, and want the moneys
very bad, you may ask double.

10 *Sir Pet.* A good honest trade you're learning, Sir
Oliver!

Sir Oliv. Truly, I think so — and not unprofitable.

Mos. Then, you know, you haven't the moneys
yourself, but are forced to borrow them for him of a
15 friend.

Sir Oliv. Oh! I borrow it of a friend, do I?

Mos. And your friend is an unconscionable dog:
but you can't help that.

Sir Oliv. My friend an unconscionable dog, is he?

20 *Mos.* Yes, and he himself has not the moneys by
him, but is forced to sell stock at a great loss.

Sir Oliv. He is forced to sell stock at a great loss,
is he? Well, that's very kind of him.

Sir Pet. I' faith, Sir Oliver — Mr. Premium, I
25 mean — you'll soon be master of the trade. But,
Moses! would not you have him run out a little

against the Annuity Bill°? That would be in character, I should think.

Mos. Very much.

Row. And lament that a young man now must be at years of discretion before he is suffered to ruin 5 himself?

Mos. Ay, great pity!

Sir Pet. And abuse the public for allowing merit to an act whose only object is to snatch misfortune and imprudence from the rapacious gripe of usury, 10 and give the minor a chance of inheriting his estate without being undone by coming into possession.

Sir Oliv. So, so — Moses shall give me farther instructions as we go together.

Sir Pet. You will not have much time, for your 15 nephew lives hard by.

Sir Oliv. Oh, never fear! my tutor appears so able, that though Charles lived in the next street, it must be my own fault if I am not a complete rogue before I turn the corner.   [*Exit with* MOSES. 20

Sir Pet. So, now, I think Sir Oliver will be convinced: you are partial, Rowley, and would have prepared Charles for the other plot.

Row. No, upon my word, Sir Peter.

Sir Pet. Well, go bring me this Snake, and I'll 25 hear what he has to say presently. I see Maria,

P

and want to speak with her. — [*Exit* ROWLEY.] I
should be glad to be convinced my suspicions of
Lady Teazle and Charles were unjust. I have never
yet opened my mind on this subject to my friend
5 Joseph — I am determined I will do it — he will
give me his opinion sincerely.

Enter MARIA

So, child, has Mr. Surface returned with you?
Mar. No, sir; he was engaged.
Sir Pet. Well, Maria, do you not reflect, the more
10 you converse with that amiable young man, what
return his partiality for you deserves?
Mar. Indeed, Sir Peter, your frequent impor-
tunity on this subject distresses me extremely —
you compel me to declare, that I know no man who
15 has ever paid me a particular attention whom I
would not prefer to Mr. Surface.
Sir Pet. So — here's perverseness! No, no, Maria,
'tis Charles only whom you would prefer. 'Tis
evident his vices and follies have won your heart.
20 *Mar.* This is unkind, sir. You know I have
obeyed you in neither seeing nor corresponding with
him: I have heard enough to convince me that he
is unworthy my regard. Yet I cannot think it

culpable, if, while my understanding severely con-
demns his vices, my heart suggests some pity for
his distresses.

Sir Pet. Well, well, pity him as much as you
please; but give your heart and hand to a worthier 5
object.

Mar. Never to his brother!

Sir Pet. Go, perverse and obstinate! But take
care, madam; you have never yet known what the
authority of a guardian is: don't compel me to in- 10
form you of it.

Mar. I can only say, you shall not have just
reason. 'Tis true, by my father's will, I am for a
short period bound to regard you as his substitute;
but must cease to think you so, when you would 15
compel me to be miserable.   [*Exit.*

Sir Pet. Was ever man so crossed as I am, every
thing conspiring to fret me! I had not been in-
volved in matrimony a fortnight, before her father,
a hale and hearty man, died, on purpose, I believe, 20
for the pleasure of plaguing me with the care
of his daughter.— [LADY TEAZLE *sings without.*]
But here comes my helpmate! She appears
in great good humour. How happy I should be
if I could tease her into loving me, though but a 25
little!

Enter LADY TEAZLE

Lady Teaz. Lud! Sir Peter, I hope you haven't been quarrelling with Maria? It is not using me well to be ill-humoured when I am not by.

Sir Pet. Ah, Lady Teazle, you might have the
5 power to make me good-humoured at all times.

Lady Teaz. I am sure I wish I had; for I want you to be in a charming sweet temper at this moment. Do be good-humoured now, and let me have two hundred pounds, will you?

10   *Sir Pet.* Two hundred pounds; what, an't I to be in a good humour without paying for it! But speak to me thus, and i' faith there's nothing I could refuse you. You shall have it; but seal me a bond for the repayment.

15   *Lady Teaz.* Oh, no — there — my note of hand will do as well.   [*Offering her hand.*

Sir Pet. And you shall no longer reproach me with not giving you an independent settlement. I mean
20 shortly to surprise you: but shall we always live thus, hey?

Lady Teaz. If you please. I'm sure I don't care how soon we leave off quarrelling, provided you'll own you were tired first.

Sir Pet. Well — then let our future contest be, who shall be most obliging.

Lady Teaz. I assure you, Sir Peter, good nature becomes you. You look now as you did before we were married, when you used to walk with me under 5 the elms, and tell me stories of what a gallant you were in your youth, and chuck me under the chin, you would; and asked me if I thought I could love an old fellow, who would deny me nothing — didn't you?   10

Sir Pet. Yes, yes, and you were as kind and attentive ——

Lady Teaz. Ay, so I was, and would always take your part, when my acquaintance used to abuse you, and turn you into ridicule.   15

Sir Pet. Indeed!

Lady Teaz. Ay, and when my cousin Sophy has called you a stiff, peevish old bachelor, and laughed at me for thinking of marrying one who might be my father, I have always defended you, and said, 20 I didn't think you so ugly by any means.

Sir Pet. Thank you.

Lady Teaz. And I dared say you'd make a very good sort of a husband.

Sir Pet. And you prophesied right; and we shall 25 now be the happiest couple ——

Lady Teaz. And never differ again?

Sir Pet. No, never! — though at the same time, indeed, my dear Lady Teazle, you must watch your temper very seriously; for in all our little quarrels, 5 my dear, if you recollect, my love, you always began first.

Lady Teaz. I beg your pardon, my dear Sir Peter: indeed, you always gave the provocation.

10   *Sir Pet.* Now see, my angel! take care — contradicting isn't the way to keep friends.

Lady Teaz. Then don't you begin it, my love!

Sir Pet. There, now! you — you are going on. You don't perceive, my life, that you are just doing 15 the very thing which you know always makes me angry.

Lady Teaz. Nay, you know, if you will be angry without any reason, my dear ——

Sir Pet. There! now you want to quarrel again.

20   *Lady Teaz.* No, I'm sure I don't: but, if you will be so peevish ——

Sir Pet. There now! who begins first?

Lady Teaz. Why, you, to be sure. I said nothing — but there's no bearing your temper.

25   *Sir Pet.* No, no, madam: the fault's in your own temper.

Lady Teaz.   Ay, you are just what my cousin
Sophy said you would be.

Sir Pet.   Your cousin Sophy is a forward, impertinent gipsy.

Lady Teaz.   You are a great bear, I'm sure, to 5
abuse my relations.

Sir Pet.   Now may all the plagues of marriage be
doubled on me, if ever I try to be friends with you
any more!

Lady Teaz.   So much the better.   10

Sir Pet.   No, no, madam: 'tis evident you never
cared a pin for me, and I was a madman to marry
you — a pert, rural coquette, that had refused half
the honest squires in the neighbourhood!

Lady Teaz.   And I am sure I was a fool to marry 15
you — an old dangling bachelor, who was single
at fifty, only because he never could meet with any
one who would have him.

Sir Pet.   Ay, ay, madam; but you were pleased
enough to listen to me: you never had such an 20
offer before.

Lady Teaz.   No! didn't I refuse Sir Tivy Terrier,
who every body said would have been a better
match? for his estate is just as good as yours, and
he has broke his neck since we have been mar- 25
ried.

Sir Pet. I have done with you, madam! You are an unfeeling, ungrateful — but there's an end of everything. I believe you capable of everything that is bad.   Yes, madam, I now believe the re-
5 ports relative to you and Charles, madam.   Yes, madam, you and Charles are, not without grounds ——

Lady Teaz. Take care, Sir Peter! you had better not insinuate any such thing!   I'll not be suspected
10 without cause, I promise you.

Sir Pet. Very well, madam! very well!   A separate maintenance as soon as you please.   Yes, madam, or a divorce!   I'll make an example of myself for the benefit of all old bachelors.   Let us separate,
15 madam.

Lady Teaz. Agreed! agreed!   And now, my dear Sir Peter, we are of a mind once more, we may be the happiest couple, and never differ again, you know: ha! ha! ha!   Well, you are going to be in
20 a passion, I see, and I shall only interrupt you — so, bye! bye!   [*Exit.*

Sir Pet. Plagues and tortures! can't I make her angry either!   Oh, I am the most miserable fellow! But I'll not bear her presuming to keep her temper:
25 no! she may break my heart, but she sha'n't keep her temper.   [*Exit.*

Scene II.   *A Room in Charles Surface's House*

Enter Trip, Moses, *and* Sir Oliver Surface

Trip. Here, Master Moses! if you'll stay a moment I'll try whether — what's the gentleman's name?

Sir Oliv. Mr. Moses, what is my name?

[*Aside to* Moses.

Mos. Mr. Premium.   5

Trip. Premium — very well.   [*Exit, taking snuff.*

Sir Oliv. To judge by the servants, one wouldn't believe the master was ruined.   But what! — sure, this was my brother's house?

Mos. Yes, sir; Mr. Charles bought it of Mr. 10 Joseph, with the furniture, pictures, &c., just as the old gentleman left it.   Sir Peter thought it a piece of extravagance in him.

Sir Oliv. In my mind, the other's economy in selling it to him was more reprehensible by half.   15

Reënter Trip

Trip. My master says you must wait, gentlemen: he has company, and can't speak with you yet.

Sir Oliv. If he knew who it was wanted to see him, perhaps he would not send such a message.

Trip. Yes, yes, sir; he knows you are here — I did not forget little Premium: no, no, no.

Sir Oliv. Very well; and I pray, sir, what may be your name?

5   *Trip.* Trip, sir; my name is Trip, at your service.

Sir Oliv. Well, then, Mr. Trip, you have a pleasant sort of place here, I guess?

Trip. Why, yes — here are three or four of us pass our time agreeably enough; but then our
10 wages are sometimes a little in arrear — and not very great either — but fifty pounds a year, and find our own bags and bouquets.

Sir Oliv. Bags and bouquets! halters and bastinadoes!   [*Aside.*

15   *Trip.* And *à propos*, Moses, have you been able to get me that little bill discounted?

Sir Oliv. Wants to raise money too! — mercy on me! Has his distresses too, I warrant, like a lord, and affects creditors and duns.   [*Aside.*

20   *Mos.* 'Twas not to be done, indeed, Mr. Trip.

Trip. Good lack, you surprise me! My friend Brush has indorsed it, and I thought when he put his name at the back of a bill 'twas the same as cash.

25   *Mos.* No, 'twouldn't do.

Trip. A small sum — but twenty pounds. Hark-

'ee, Moses, do you think you couldn't get it me by way of annuity?

Sir Oliv. An annuity! ha! ha! a footman raise money by way of annuity! Well done, luxury, egad!   [*Aside.* 5

Mos. Well, but you must insure your place.

Trip. Oh, with all my heart! I'll insure my place, and my life too, if you please.

Sir Oliv. It's more than I would your neck.
                                                [*Aside.*

Mos. But is there nothing you could deposit?   10

Trip. Why, nothing capital of my master's wardrobe has dropped lately; but I could give you a mortgage on some of his winter clothes, with equity of redemption before November — or you shall have the reversion of the French velvet, or a post-obit° 15 on the blue and silver; — these, I should think, Moses, with a few pair of point ruffles, as a collateral security — hey, my little fellow?

Mos. Well, well.   [*Bell rings.*

Trip. Egad, I heard the bell! I believe, gentle- 20 men, I can now introduce you. Don't forget the annuity, little Moses! This way, gentlemen, I'll insure my place, you know.

Sir Oliv. [*Aside.*] If the man be a shadow of the master, this is the temple of dissipation indeed!   25
                                                [*Exeunt.*

SCENE III.   *Another Room in the same*

CHARLES SURFACE, SIR HARRY BUMPER, CARELESS,
    and GENTLEMEN, *discovered drinking*

Chas. Surf. 'Fore heaven, 'tis true! — there's the
great degeneracy of the age.   Many of our acquaintance have taste, spirit, and politeness; but, plague
on't, they won't drink.

5   *Care.* It is so, indeed, Charles! they give in to all
the substantial luxuries of the table, and abstain
from nothing but wine and wit.   Oh, certainly
society suffers by it intolerably! for now, instead of
the social spirit of raillery that used to mantle over
10 a glass of bright Burgundy, their conversation is
become just like the Spa-water they drink, which has
all the pertness and flatulency of champagne, without its spirit or flavour.

1 *Gent.* But what are they to do who love play
15 better than wine?

Care. True! there's Sir Harry diets himself for
gaming, and is now under a hazard regimen.

Chas. Surf. Then he'll have the worst of it.
What! you wouldn't train a horse for the course by
20 keeping him from corn? For my part, egad, I
am never so successful as when I am a little merry:

let me throw on a bottle of champagne, and I never lose.

All. Hey, what?

Care. At least I never feel my losses, which is exactly the same thing.   5

2 *Gent.* Ay, that I believe.

Chas. Surf. And then, what man can pretend to be a believer in love, who is an abjurer of wine? 'Tis the test by which the lover knows his own heart. Fill a dozen bumpers to a dozen beauties, and she 10 that floats at the top is the maid that has bewitched you.

Care. Now then, Charles, be honest, and give us your real favourite.

Chas. Surf. Why, I have withheld her only in 15 compassion to you. If I toast her, you must give a round of her peers, which is impossible — on earth.

Care. Oh! then we'll find some canonised vestals or heathen goddesses that will do, I warrant!   20

Chas. Surf. Here then, bumpers, you rogues! bumpers! Maria! Maria! ——

Sir Har. Maria who?

Chas. Surf. Oh, damn the surname! — 'tis too formal to be registered in Love's calendar — 25 Maria!

All. Maria!

Chas. Surf. But now, Sir Harry, beware, we must have beauty superlative.

Care. Nay, never study, Sir Harry: we'll stand
5 to the toast, though your mistress should want an eye, and you know you have a song will excuse you.

Sir Har. Egad, so I have! and I'll give him the song instead of the lady.   [*Sings.*

Here's to the maiden of bashful fifteen;
10   Here's to the widow of fifty;
Here's to the flaunting extravagant quean,
    And here's to the housewife that's thrifty.
Chorus. Let the toast pass, —
        Drink to the lass,
15 I'll warrant she'll prove an excuse for the glass.

Here's to the charmer whose dimples we prize;
    Now to the maid who has none, sir:
Here's to the girl with a pair of blue eyes,
    And here's to the nymph with but one, sir.
20 *Chorus.* Let the toast pass, &c.

Here's to the maid with a bosom of snow:
    Now to her that's as brown as a berry:
Here's to the wife with a face full of woe,
    And now to the damsel that's merry.
25 *Chorus.* Let the toast pass, &c.

For let 'em be clumsy, or let 'em be slim,
   Young or ancient, I care not a feather;
So fill a pint bumper quite up to the brim,
   So fill up your glasses, nay, fill to the brim,
And let us e'en toast them together.   5
Chorus. Let the toast pass, &c.

All. Bravo! bravo!

Enter TRIP, *and whispers* CHARLES SURFACE

Chas. Surf. Gentlemen, you must excuse me a
little. — Careless, take the chair, will you?
Care. Nay, pr'ythee, Charles, what now? This 10
is one of your peerless beauties, I suppose, has
dropped in by chance?
Chas. Surf. No, faith! To tell you the truth,
'tis a Jew and a broker, who are come by appointment.   15
Care. Oh! let's have the Jew in.
1 Gent. Ay, and the broker too, by all means.
2 Gent. Yes, yes, the Jew and the broker.
Chas. Surf. Egad, with all my heart! — Trip, bid
the gentlemen walk in. — [*Exit* TRIP.] Though 20
there's one of them a stranger, I can tell you.
Care. Charles, let us give them some generous
Burgundy, and perhaps they'll grow conscientious.

Chas. Surf. Oh, hang 'em, no! wine does but draw forth a man's natural qualities; and to make them drink would only be to whet their knavery.

Reënter TRIP, *with* SIR OLIVER SURFACE *and* MOSES

Chas. Surf. So, honest Moses; walk in, pray, 5 Mr. Premium — that's the gentleman's name, isn't it, Moses?

Mos. Yes, sir.

Chas. Surf. Set chairs, Trip. — Sit down, Mr. Premium. — Glasses, Trip. — [TRIP *gives chairs and* 10 *glasses, and exit.*] Sit down, Moses. — Come, Mr. Premium, I'll give you a sentiment; here's *Success to usury!* — Moses, fill the gentleman a bumper.

Mos. Success to usury!   [*Drinks.*

Care. Right, Moses — usury is prudence and 15 industry, and deserves to succeed.

Sir Oliv. Then here's — All the success it deserves!
                                            [*Drinks.*

Care. No, no, that won't do! Mr. Premium, you have demurred at the toast, and must drink it in a pint bumper.

20 1 *Gent.* A pint bumper, at least.

Mos. Oh, pray, sir, consider — Mr. Premium's a gentleman.

Care. And therefore loves good wine.

2 *Gent.* Give Moses a quart glass — this is mutiny, and a high contempt for the chair.

Care. Here, now for't! I'll see justice done to the last drop of my bottle.   5

Sir Oliv. Nay, pray, gentlemen — I did not expect this usage.

Chas. Surf. No, hang it, you shan't; Mr. Premium's a stranger.

Sir Oliv. Odd! I wish I was well out of their 10 company.   [*Aside.*

Care. Plague on 'em then! if they won't drink, we'll not sit down with them. Come, Harry, the dice are in the next room. — Charles, you'll join us when you have finished your business with the 15 gentlemen?

Chas. Surf. I will! I will! — [*Exeunt* Sir Harry Bumper *and* Gentlemen; Careless *following*.] Careless!

Care. [*Returning.*] Well!   20

Chas. Surf. Perhaps I may want you.

Care. Oh, you know I am always ready: word, note, or bond, 'tis all the same to me.   [*Exit.*

Mos. Sir, this is Mr. Premium, a gentleman of the strictest honour and secrecy; and always per- 25 forms what he undertakes. Mr. Premium, this is ——

Q

Chas. Surf. Pshaw! have done. Sir, my friend
Moses is a very honest fellow, but a little slow at
expression: he'll be an hour giving us our titles.
Mr. Premium, the plain state of the matter is this:
5 I am an extravagant young fellow who wants to
borrow money; you I take to be a prudent old
fellow, who have got money to lend. I am blockhead enough to give fifty per cent. sooner than not
have it; and you, I presume, are rogue enough to
10 take a hundred if you can get it. Now, sir, you
see we are acquainted at once, and may proceed to
business without farther ceremony.

Sir Oliv. Exceeding frank, upon my word. I
see, sir, you are not a man of many compliments.

15   *Chas. Surf.* Oh, no, sir! plain dealing in business
I always think best.

Sir Oliv. Sir, I like you the better for it. However, you are mistaken in one thing; I have no
money to lend, but I believe I could procure some
20 of a friend; but then he's an unconscionable dog.
Isn't he, Moses? And must sell stock to accommodate you. Mustn't he, Moses?

Mos. Yes, indeed! You know I always speak
the truth, and scorn to tell a lie!

25   *Chas. Surf.* Right. People that speak truth
generally do. But these are trifles, Mr. Premium.

What! I know money isn't to be bought without
paying for't!

Sir Oliv. Well, but what security could you give?
You have no land, I suppose?

Chas. Surf. Not a mole-hill, nor a twig, but what's 5
in the bough-pots out of the window!

Sir Oliv. Nor any stock, I presume?

Chas. Surf. Nothing but live stock — and that's
only a few pointers and ponies. But pray, Mr.
Premium, are you acquainted at all with any of 10
my connections?

Sir Oliv. Why, to say truth, I am.

Chas. Surf. Then you must know that I have a
devilish rich uncle in the East Indies, Sir Oliver
Surface, from whom I have the greatest expecta- 15
tions?

Sir Oliv. That you have a wealthy uncle, I have
heard; but how your expectations will turn out is
more, I believe, than you can tell.

Chas. Surf. Oh, no! — there can be no doubt. 20
They tell me I'm a prodigious favourite, and that
he talks of leaving me every thing.

Sir Oliv. Indeed! this is the first I've heard of it.

Chas. Surf. Yes, yes, 'tis just so. Moses knows
'tis true; don't you, Moses?   25

Mos. Oh, yes! I'll swear to't.

Sir Oliv. Egad, they'll persuade me presently I'm
at Bengal.   [*Aside.*

Chas. Surf. Now I propose, Mr. Premium, if it's
agreeable to you, a post-obit on Sir Oliver's life:
5 though at the same time the old fellow has been so
liberal to me, that I give you my word, I should be
very sorry to hear that anything had happened to him.

Sir Oliv. Not more than I should, I assure you.
But the bond you mention happens to be just the
10 worst security you could offer me — for I might
live to a hundred and never see the principal.

Chas. Surf. Oh, yes, you would! the moment Sir
Oliver dies, you know, you would come on me for
the money.

15 *Sir Oliv.* Then I believe I should be the most
unwelcome dun you ever had in your life.

Chas. Surf. What! I suppose you're afraid that
Sir Oliver is too good a life?

Sir Oliv. No, indeed I am not; though I have
20 heard he is as hale and healthy as any man of his
years in Christendom.

Chas. Surf. There again, now, you are misinformed. No, no, the climate has hurt him con-
siderably, poor uncle Oliver. Yes, yes, he breaks
25 apace, I'm told — and is so much altered lately that
his nearest relations would not know him.

Sir Oliv. No! Ha! ha! ha! so much altered
lately that his nearest relations would not know
him! Ha! ha! ha! egad — ha! ha! ha!

Chas. Surf. Ha! ha! — you're glad to hear that,
little Premium?   5

Sir Oliv. No, no, I'm not.

Chas. Surf. Yes, yes, you are — ha! ha! ha! —
you know that mends your chance.

Sir Oliv. But I'm told Sir Oliver is coming over;
nay, some say he is actually arrived.   10

Chas. Surf. Pshaw! sure I must know better
than you whether he's come or not. No, no, rely
on't he's at this moment at Calcutta. Isn't he,
Moses?

Mos. Oh, yes, certainly.   15

Sir Oliv. Very true, as you say, you must know
better than I, though I have it from pretty good
authority. Haven't I, Moses?

Mos. Yes, most undoubted!

Sir Oliv. But, sir, as I understand you want a   20
few hundreds immediately, is there nothing you
could dispose of?

Chas. Surf. How do you mean?

Sir Oliv. For instance, now, I have heard that
your father left behind him a great quantity of   25
massy old plate.

Chas. Surf. O Lud! that's gone long ago. Moses can tell you how better than I can.

Sir Oliv. [*Aside.*] Good lack! all the family race-cups and corporation-bowls°! — [*Aloud.*] Then
5 it was also supposed that his library was one of the most valuable and compact.

Chas. Surf. Yes, yes, so it was — vastly too much so for a private gentleman. For my part, I was always of a communicative disposition, so I thought
10 it a shame to keep so much knowledge to myself.

Sir Oliv. [*Aside.*] Mercy upon me! learning that had run in the family like an heir-loom! — [*Aloud.*] Pray, what are become of the books?

Chas. Surf. You must inquire of the auctioneer,
15 Master Premium, for I don't believe even Moses can direct you.

Mos. I know nothing of books.

Sir Oliv. So, so, nothing of the family property left, I suppose?

20 *Chas. Surf.* Not much, indeed; unless you have a mind to the family pictures. I have got a room full of ancestors above; and if you have a taste for old paintings, egad, you shall have 'em a bargain!

25 *Sir Oliv.* Hey! what the devil! sure, you wouldn't sell your forefathers, would you?

Chas. Surf. Every man of them, to the best bidder.

Sir Oliv. What! your great-uncles and aunts?

Chas. Surf. Ay, and my great-grandfathers and grandmothers too.   5

Sir Oliv. [*Aside.*] Now I give him up! — [*Aloud.*] What the plague, have you no bowels for your own kindred? Odds life! do you take me for Shylock in the play, that you would raise money of me on your own flesh and blood?   10

Chas. Surf. Nay, my little broker, don't be angry: what need you care, if you have your money's worth?

Sir Oliv. Well, I'll be the purchaser: I think I can dispose of the family canvas. — [*Aside.*] Oh, 15 I'll never forgive him this! never!

Reënter CARELESS

Care. Come, Charles, what keeps you?

Chas. Surf. I can't come yet. I' faith, we are going to have a sale above stairs; here's little Premium will buy all my ancestors!   20

Care. Oh, burn your ancestors!

Chas. Surf. No, he may do that afterwards, if he pleases. Stay, Careless, we want you: egad, you shall be auctioneer — so come along with us.

Care. Oh, have with you, if that's the case. I can handle a hammer as well as a dice-box! Going! going!

Sir Oliv. Oh, the profligates!   [*Aside.*

5   *Chas. Surf.* Come, Moses, you shall be appraiser, if we want one. Gad's life, little Premium, you don't seem to like the business?

Sir Oliv. Oh, yes, I do, vastly! Ha! ha! ha! yes, yes, I think it a rare joke to sell one's family

10 by auction — ha! ha! — [*Aside.*] Oh, the prodigal!

Chas. Surf. To be sure! when a man wants money, where the plague should he get assistance, if he can't make free with his own relations!

[*Exeunt.*

Sir Oliv. I'll never forgive him; never! never!

ACT IV

SCENE I. *A Picture Room in Charles Surface's House*

Enter CHARLES SURFACE, SIR OLIVER SURFACE, MOSES, *and* CARELESS

Chas. Surf. Walk in, gentlemen, pray walk in; — here they are, the family of the Surfaces, up to the Conquest.

Sir Oliv. And, in my opinion, a goodly collection.

Chas. Surf. Ay, ay, these are done in the true 5 spirit of portrait-painting; no *volontière grace*° or expression. Not like the works of your modern Raphaels, who give you the strongest resemblance, yet contrive to make your portrait independent of you; so that you may sink the original and not hurt 10 the picture. No, no; the merit of these is the inveterate likeness — all stiff and awkward as the originals, and like nothing in human nature besidés.

Sir Oliv. Ah! we shall never see such figures of men again. 15

Chas. Surf. I' hope not. Well, you see, Master Premium, what a domestic character I am; here

I sit of an evening surrounded by my family. But come, get to your pulpit, Mr. Auctioneer; here's an old gouty chair of my grandfather's will answer the purpose.

5 *Care.* Ay, ay, this will do. But, Charles, I haven't a hammer; and what's an auctioneer without his hammer?

Chas. Surf. Egad, that's true. What parchment have we here? Oh, our genealogy in full. [*Taking*
10 *pedigree down.*] Here, Careless, you shall have no common bit of mahogany, here's the family tree for you, you rogue! This shall be your hammer, and now you may knock down my ancestors with their own pedigree.

15 *Sir Oliv.* What an unnatural rogue! — an *ex post facto*° parricide!   [*Aside.*

Care. Yes, yes, here's a list of your generation indeed; — faith, Charles, this is the most convenient thing you could have found for the business,
20 for 'twill not only serve as a hammer, but a catalogue into the bargain. Come, begin — A-going, a-going, a-going!

Chas. Surf. Bravo, Careless! Well, here's my great-uncle, Sir Richard Raveline, a marvellous
25 good general in his day, I assure you. He served in all the Duke of Marlborough's° wars, and got that

cut over his eye at the battle of Malplaquet.° What
say you, Mr. Premium? look at him — there's
a hero! not cut out of his feathers, as your modern clipped captains are, but enveloped in wig and
regimentals, as a general should be. What do you 5
bid?

Sir Oliv. [*Aside to Moses.*] Bid him speak.

Mos. Mr. Premium would have you speak.

Chas. Surf. Why, then, he shall have him for
ten pounds, and I'm sure that's not dear for a staff- 10
officer.

Sir Oliver. [*Aside.*] Heaven deliver me! his
famous uncle Richard for ten pounds! — [*Aloud.*]
Very well, sir, I take him at that.

Chas. Surf. Careless, knock down my uncle 15
Richard. — Here, now, is a maiden sister of his, my
great-aunt Deborah, done by Kneller,° in his best
manner, and esteemed a very formidable likeness.
There she is, you see, a shepherdess feeding her flock.
You shall have her for five pounds ten — the sheep 20
are worth the money.

Sir Oliv. [*Aside.*] Ah! poor Deborah! a woman
who set such a value on herself! — [*Aloud.*] Five
pounds ten — she's mine.

Chas. Surf. Knock down my aunt Deborah! 25
Here, now, are two that were a sort of cousins of

theirs. — You see, Moses, these pictures were done some time ago, when beaux wore wigs, and the ladies their own hair.

Sir Oliv. Yes, truly, head-dresses appear to have
5 been a little lower in those days.

Chas. Surf. Well, take that couple for the same.

Mos. 'Tis a good bargain.

Chas. Surf. Careless! — This, now, is a grandfather of my mother's, a learned judge, well known
10 on the western circuit. — What do you rate him at, Moses?

Mos. Four guineas.

Chas. Surf. Four guineas! Gad's life, you don't bid me the price of his wig. — Mr. Premium, you
15 have more respect for the woolsack°; do let us knock his lordship down at fifteen.

Sir Oliv. By all means.

Care. Gone! .

Chas. Surf. And there are two brothers of his,
20 William and Walter Blunt, Esquires, both members of parliament, and noted speakers; and, what's very extraordinary, I believe, this is the first time they were ever bought or sold.

Sir Oliv. That is very extraordinary, indeed!
25 I'll take them at your own price, for the honour of parliament.

Care. Well said, little Premium! I'll knock them down at forty.

Chas. Surf. Here's a jolly fellow — I don't know what relation, but he was mayor of Norwich: take him at eight pounds. 5

Sir Oliv. No, no; six will do for the mayor.

Chas. Surf. Come, make it guineas, and I'll throw you the two aldermen there into the bargain.

Sir Oliv. They're mine.

Chas. Surf. Careless, knock down the mayor and 10 aldermen. But, plague on't! we shall be all day retailing in this manner; do let us deal wholesale: what say you, little Premium? Give me three hundred pounds for the rest of the family in the lump. 15

Care. Ay, ay, that will be the best way.

Sir Oliv. Well, well, any thing to accommodate you; they are mine. But there is one portrait which you have always passed over.

Care. What, that ill-looking little fellow over the 20 settee.

Sir Oliv. Yes, sir, I mean that; though I don't think him so ill-looking a little fellow, by any means.

Chas. Surf. What, that? Oh; that's my uncle Oliver! 'twas done before he went to India. 25

Care. Your uncle Oliver! Gad, then you'll never

be friends, Charles. That, now, to me, is as stern
a looking rogue as ever I saw; an unforgiving
eye, and a disinheriting countenance! an inveterate
knave, depend on't. Don't you think so, little
5 Premium?

Sir Oliv. Upon my soul, sir, I do not; I think it
is as honest a looking face as any in the room, dead
or alive. But I suppose uncle Oliver goes with the
rest of the lumber?

10   *Chas. Surf.* No, hang it! I'll not part with poor
Noll. The old fellow has been very good to me, and,
egad, I'll keep his picture while I've a room to put
it in.

Sir Oliv. [*Aside.*] The rogue's my nephew after
15 all! — [*Aloud.*] But, sir, I have somehow taken a
fancy to that picture.

Chas. Surf. I'm sorry for't, for you certainly
will not have it. Oons, haven't you got enough of
them?

20   *Sir Oliv.* [*Aside.*] I forgive him every thing! —
[*Aloud.*] But, sir, when I take a whim in my head,
I don't value money. I'll give you as much for
that as for all the rest.

Chas. Surf. Don't tease me, master broker; I
25 tell you I'll not part with it, and there's an end
of it.

Sir Oliv. [*Aside.*]   How like his father the dog
is! — [*Aloud.*]   Well, well, I have done. — [*Aside.*]
I did not perceive it before, but I think I never
saw such a striking resemblance. — [*Aloud.*] Here
is a draft for your sum.   5
   Chas. Surf. Why, 'tis for eight hundred pounds!
   Sir Oliv. You will not let Sir Oliver go?
   Chas. Surf. Zounds! no! I tell you, once more.
   Sir Oliv. Then never mind the difference, we'll
balance that another time.   But give me your 10
hand on the bargain; you are an honest fellow,
Charles — I beg pardon, sir, for being so free.
— Come, Moses.
   Chas. Surf. Egad, this is a whimsical old fellow!
— But hark'ee, Premium, you'll prepare lodgings 15
for these gentlemen.
   Sir Oliv. Yes, yes, I'll send for them in a day or
two.
   Chas. Surf. But hold; do now send a genteel
conveyance for them, for, I assure you, they were 20
most of them used to ride in their own carriages.
   Sir Oliv. I will, I will — for all but Oliver.
   Chas. Surf. Ay, all but the little nabob.
   Sir Oliv. You're fixed on that?
   Chas. Surf. Peremptorily.   25
   Sir Oliv. [*Aside.*]   A dear extravagant rogue!

— [*Aloud.*]   Good day ! — Come, Moses. — [*Aside.*]
Let me hear now who dares call him profligate.
[*Exit with* MOSES.
   Care. Why, this is the oddest genius of the sort
I ever met with !
5   *Chas. Surf.* Egad, he's the prince of brokers,
I think. I wonder how the devil Moses got acquainted with so honest a fellow. — Ha ! here's
Rowley. — Do, Careless, say I'll join the company
in a few moments.
10   *Care.* I will — but don't let that old blockhead persuade you to squander any of that
money on old musty debts, or any such nonsense;
for tradesmen, Charles, are the most exorbitant
fellows.
15   *Chas. Surf.* Very true, and paying them is only
encouraging them.
   Care. Nothing else.
   Chas. Surf. Ay, ay, never fear. — [*Exit* CARE-
LESS.] So ! this was an odd old fellow, indeed.
20 Let me see, two-thirds of these five hundred and
thirty odd pounds are mine by right. 'Fore
heaven ! I find one's ancestors are more valuable
relations than I took them for ! — Ladies and
gentlemen, your most obedient and very grateful
25 servant.   [*Bows ceremoniously to the pictures.*

Enter ROWLEY

Ha! old Rowley! egad, you are just come in time
to take leave of your old acquaintance.

Row. Yes, I heard they were a-going. But I
wonder you can have such spirits under so many
distresses.   5

Chas. Surf. Why, there's the point! my distresses are so many, that I can't afford to part
with my spirits; but I shall be rich and splenetic,
all in good time. However, I suppose you are
surprised that I am not more sorrowful at parting 10
with so many near relations; to be sure, 'tis very
affecting, but you see they never move a muscle,
so why should I?

Row. There's no making you serious a moment.

Chas. Surf. Yes, faith, I am so now. Here, 15
my honest Rowley, here, get me this changed
directly, and take a hundred pounds of it immediately to old Stanley.

Row. A hundred pounds! Consider only ——

Chas. Surf. Gad's life, don't talk about it! poor 20
Stanley's wants are pressing, and, if you don't
make haste, we shall have some one call that has
a better right to the money.

Row. Ah! there's the point! I never will cease
dunning you with the old proverb ——   25

R

Chas. Surf. Be just before you're generous. —
Why, so I would if I could; but Justice is an old,
hobbling beldame, and I can't get her to keep
pace with Generosity, for the soul of me.

5   *Row.* Yet, Charles, believe me, one hour's reflection ——

Chas. Surf. Ay, ay, it's very true; but, hark'ee,
Rowley, while I have, by Heaven I'll give; and
now for hazard.   [*Exeunt.*

SCENE II.   *Another Room in the same*

Enter SIR OLIVER SURFACE *and* MOSES

10   *Mos.* Well, sir, I think, as Sir Peter said, you
have seen Mr. Charles in high glory; 'tis great
pity he's so extravagant.

Sir Oliv. True, but he would not sell my picture.

Mos. And loves wine and women so much.

15   *Sir Oliv.* But he would not sell my picture.

Mos. And games so deep.

Sir Oliv. But he would not sell my picture. Oh,
here's Rowley.

Enter ROWLEY

Row. So, Sir Oliver, I find you have made a
20 purchase ——

Sir Oliv. Yes, yes, our young rake has parted with his ancestors like old tapestry.

Row. And here has he commissioned me to re-deliver you part of the purchase money — I mean, though, in your necessitous character of old Stanley. 5

Mos. Ah! there is the pity of all; he is so charitable.

Row. And I left a hosier and two tailors in the hall, who, I'm sure, won't be paid, and this hundred would satisfy them. 10

Sir Oliv. Well, well, I'll pay his debts, and his benevolence too. But now I am no more a broker, and you shall introduce me to the elder brother as old Stanley.

Row. Not yet awhile; Sir Peter, I know, means 15 to call there about this time.

Enter TRIP

Trip. Oh, gentlemen, I beg pardon for not show-ing you out; this way — Moses, a word.

[*Exit with* MOSES.

Sir Oliv. There's a fellow for you! Would you believe it, that puppy intercepted the Jew on our 20 coming, and wanted to raise money before he got to his master!

Row. Indeed!

Sir Oliv. Yes, they are now planning an annuity business. Ah, Master Rowley, in my days servants were content with the follies of their masters,
5 when they were worn a little threadbare; but now they have their vices, like their birthday clothes, with the gloss on.   [*Exeunt.*

SCENE III. *A Library in Joseph Surface's House*

Enter JOSEPH SURFACE *and* SERVANT

Jos. Surf. No letter from Lady Teazle?

Ser. No, sir.

10 *Jos. Surf.* [*Aside.*] I am surprised she has not sent, if she is prevented from coming. Sir Peter certainly does not suspect me. Yet I wish I may not lose the heiress, through the scrape I have drawn myself into with the wife; however, Charles's
15 imprudence and bad character are great points in my favour.   [*Knocking without.*

Ser. Sir, I believe that must be Lady Teazle.

Jos. Surf. Hold! See whether it is or not, before you go to the door: I have a particular
20 message for you if it should be my brother.

Ser. 'Tis her ladyship, sir; she always leaves her chair at the milliner's in the next street.

Jos. Surf. Stay, stay; draw that screen before the window — that will do; — my opposite neighbour is a maiden lady of so curious a temper. — [SERVANT *draws the screen, and exit.*] I have a difficult hand to play in this affair. Lady Teazle has 5 lately suspected my views on Maria; but she must by no means be let into that secret, — at least, till I have her more in my power.

Enter LADY TEAZLE

Lady Teaz. What, sentiment in soliloquy now? Have you been very impatient? O Lud! don't 10 pretend to look grave. I vow I couldn't come before.

Jos. Surf. O madam, punctuality is a species of constancy very unfashionable in a lady of quality.

[*Places chairs, and sits after* LADY TEAZLE *is seated.*

Lady Teaz. Upon my word, you ought to pity 15 me. Do you know Sir Peter is grown so ill-natured to me of late, and so jealous of Charles too — that's the best of the story, isn't it?

Jos. Surf. I am glad my scandalous friends keep that up. [*Aside.* 20

Lady Teaz. I am sure I wish he would let Maria marry him, and then perhaps he would be convinced; don't you, Mr. Surface?

Jos. Surf. [*Aside.*] Indeed I do not. — [*Aloud.*]
Oh, certainly I do! for then my dear Lady Teazle
would also be convinced how wrong her suspicions
were of my having any design on the silly girl.

5 *Lady Teaz.* Well, well, I'm inclined to believe
you. But isn't it provoking, to have the most
ill-natured things said of one? And there's my
friend Lady Sneerwell has circulated I don't know
how many scandalous tales of me, and all without
10 any foundation too; that's what vexes me.

Jos. Surf. Ay, madam, to be sure, that is the
provoking circumstance — without foundation;
yes, yes, there's the mortification, indeed; for
when a scandalous story is believed against one,
15 there certainly is no comfort like the consciousness
of having deserved it.

Lady Teaz. No, to be sure, then I'd forgive
their malice; but to attack me, who am really so
innocent, and who never say an ill-natured thing
20 of any body — that is, of any friend; and then
Sir Peter, too, to have him so peevish, and so
suspicious, when I know the integrity of my own
heart — indeed 'tis monstrous!

Jos. Surf. But, my dear Lady Teazle, 'tis your
25 own fault if you suffer it. When a husband entertains a groundless suspicion of his wife, and

withdraws his confidence from her, the original
compact is broken, and she owes it to the honour
of her sex to endeavour to outwit him.

Lady Teaz. Indeed! So that, if he suspects me
without cause, it follows, that the best way of 5
curing his jealousy is to give him reason for't?

Jos. Surf. Undoubtedly — for your husband
should never be deceived in you: and in that case
it becomes you to be frail in compliment to his
discernment.   10

Lady Teaz. To be sure, what you say is very
reasonable, and when the consciousness of my
innocence ——

Jos. Surf. Ah, my dear madam, there is the
great mistake! 'tis this very conscious innocence 15
that is of the greatest prejudice to you. What is
it makes you negligent of forms, and careless of
the world's opinion? why, the consciousness of
your own innocence. What makes you thought-
less in your conduct, and apt to run into a thousand 20
little imprudences? why, the consciousness of your
own innocence. What makes you impatient of
Sir Peter's temper, and outrageous at his suspicions? why, the consciousness of your innocence.

Lady Teaz. 'Tis very true!   25

Jos. Surf. Now, my dear Lady Teazle, if you

would but once make a trifling *faux pas*, you can't
conceive how cautious you would grow, and how
ready to humour and agree with your husband.

    Lady Teaz. Do you think so?

5   *Jos. Surf.* Oh, I am sure on't; and then you
would find all scandal would cease at once, for —
in short, your character at present is like a person
in a plethora, absolutely dying from too much
health.

10 *Lady Teaz.* So, so; then I perceive your pre-
scription is, that I must sin in my own defence,
and part with my virtue to preserve my reputation?

    Jos. Surf. Exactly so, upon my credit, ma'am.

    Lady Teaz. Well, certainly this is the oddest doc-
15 trine, and the newest receipt for avoiding calumny!

    Jos. Surf. An infallible one, believe me. Pru-
dence, like experience, must be paid for.

    Lady Teaz. Why, if my understanding were
once convinced ——

20 *Jos. Surf.* Oh, certainly, madam, your understanding should be convinced. Yes, yes — Heaven
forbid I should persuade you to do any thing you
thought wrong. No, no, I have too much honour
to desire it.

25 *Lady Teaz.* Don't you think we may as well
leave honour out of the argument?   [*Rises.*

Jos. Surf. Ah, the ill effects of your country education, I see, still remain with you.

Lady Teaz. I doubt they do indeed; and I will fairly own to you, that if I could be persuaded to do wrong, it would be by Sir Peter's ill usage 5 sooner than your honourable logic, after all.

Jos. Surf. Then, by this hand, which he is unworthy of ——   [*Taking her hand.*

Reënter SERVANT

'Sdeath, you blockhead — what do you want?

Ser. I beg your pardon, sir, but I thought you 10 would not choose Sir Peter to come up without announcing him.

Jos. Surf. Sir Peter! — Oons — the devil!

Lady Teaz. Sir Peter! O Lud! I'm ruined! I'm ruined!   15

Ser. Sir, 'twasn't I let him in.

Lady Teaz. Oh! I'm quite undone! What will become of me? Now, Mr. Logic — Oh! mercy, sir, he's on the stairs — I'll get behind here — and if ever I'm so imprudent again ——   20
                      [*Goes behind the screen.*

Jos. Surf. Give me that book.
[*Sits down.* SERVANT *pretends to adjust his chair.*

Enter SIR PETER TEAZLE

Sir Pet. Ay, ever improving himself — Mr. Surface, Mr. Surface ——

[*Pats* JOSEPH *on the shoulder.*

Jos. Surf. Oh, my dear Sir Peter, I beg your
pardon. — [*Gaping, throws away the book.*] I have
5 been dozing over a stupid book. Well, I am
much obliged to you for this call. You haven't
been here, I believe, since I fitted up this room.
Books, you know, are the only things I am a coxcomb in.

10 *Sir Pet.* 'Tis very neat indeed. Well, well,
that's proper; and you can make even your screen
a source of knowledge — hung, I perceive, with
maps.

Jos. Surf. Oh, yes, I find great use in that
15 screen.

Sir Pet. I dare say you must, certainly, when
you want to find any thing in a hurry.

Jos. Surf. Ay, or to hide any thing in a hurry
either.   [*Aside.*

20 *Sir Pet.* Well, I have a little private business ——

Jos. Surf. You need not stay.   [*To* SERVANT.

Ser. No, sir.   [*Exit.*

Jos. Surf. Here's a chair, Sir Peter — I beg ——

Sir Pet. Well, now we are alone, there is a subject, my dear friend, on which I wish to unburden
my mind to you — a point of the greatest moment
to my peace; in short, my good friend, Lady
Teazle's conduct of late has made me very unhappy. 5

Jos. Surf. Indeed! I am very sorry to hear it.

Sir Pet. 'Tis but too plain she has not the least
regard for me; but, what's worse, I have pretty
good authority to suppose she has formed an
attachment to another.   10

Jos. Surf. Indeed! you astonish me!

Sir Pet. Yes! and, between ourselves, I think
I've discovered the person.

Jos. Surf. How! you alarm me exceedingly.

Sir Pet. Ay, my dear friend, I knew you would 15
sympathise with me!

Jos. Surf. Yes, believe me, Sir Peter, such a
discovery would hurt me just as much as it would
you.

Sir Pet. I am convinced of it. Ah! it is a hap- 20
piness to have a friend whom we can trust even
with one's family secrets. But have you no guess
who I mean?

Jos. Surf. I haven't the most distant idea. It
can't be Sir Benjamin Backbite!   25

Sir Pet. Oh, no! What say you to Charles?

Jos. Surf. My brother! impossible!

Sir Pet. Oh, my dear friend, the goodness of your own heart misleads you. You judge of others by yourself.

5   *Jos. Surf.* Certainly, Sir Peter, the heart that is conscious of its own integrity is ever slow to credit another's treachery.

Sir Pet. True; but your brother has no sentiment — you never hear him talk so.

10   *Jos. Surf.* Yet I can't but think Lady Teazle herself has too much principle.

Sir Pet. Ay; but what is principle against the flattery of a handsome, lively young fellow?

Jos. Surf. That's very true.

15   *Sir Pet.* And then, you know, the difference of our ages makes it very improbable that she should have any great affection for me; and if she were to be frail, and I were to make it public, why the town would only laugh at me, the foolish old bache-
20 lor, who had married a girl.

Jos. Surf. That's true, to be sure — they would laugh.

Sir Pet. Laugh! ay, and make ballads, and paragraphs, and the devil knows what of me.

25   *Jos. Surf.* No, you must never make it public.

Sir Pet. But then again — that the nephew

of my old friend, Sir Oliver, should be the person to attempt such a wrong, hurts me more
nearly.

Jos. Surf. Ay, there's the point. When ingratitude barbs the dart of injury, the wound has 5
double danger in it.

Sir Pet. Ay — I, that was, in a manner, left
his guardian; in whose house he had been so often
entertained; who never in my life denied him —
my advice!   10

Jos. Surf. Oh, 'tis not to be credited! There
may be a man capable of such baseness, to be sure;
but, for my part, till you can give me positive
proofs, I cannot but doubt it. However, if it
should be proved on him, he is no longer a brother 15
of mine — I disclaim kindred with him: for the
man who can break the laws of hospitality, and
tempt the wife of his friend, deserves to be branded
as the pest of society.

Sir Pet. What a difference there is between you! 20
What noble sentiments!

Jos. Surf. Yet I cannot suspect Lady Teazle's
honour.

Sir Pet. I am sure I wish to think well of her,
and to remove all ground of quarrel between us. 25
She has lately reproached me more than once

with having made no settlement on her; and, in our last quarrel, she almost hinted that she should not break her heart if I was dead. Now, as we seem to differ in our ideas of expense, I have 5 resolved she shall have her own way, and be her own mistress in that respect for the future; and, if I were to die, she will find I have not been inattentive to her interest while living. Here, my friend, are the drafts of two deeds, which I wish 10 to have your opinion on. By one, she will enjoy eight hundred a year independent while I live; and, by the other, the bulk of my fortune at my death.

Jos. Surf. This conduct, Sir Peter, is indeed 15 truly generous. — [*Aside.*] I wish it may not corrupt my pupil.

Sir Pet. Yes, I am determined she shall have no cause to complain, though I would not have her acquainted with the latter instance of my 20 affection yet awhile.

Jos. Surf. Nor I, if I could help it.   [*Aside.*

Sir Pet. And now, my dear friend, if you please, we will talk over the situation of your hopes with Maria.

25 *Jos. Surf.* [*Softly.*] Oh, no, Sir Peter; another time, if you please.

Sir Pet. I am sensibly chagrined at the little progress you seem to make in her affections.

Jos. Surf. [*Softly.*] I beg you will not mention it. What are my disappointments when your happiness is in debate! — [*Aside.*] 'Sdeath, I 5 shall be ruined every way!

Sir Pet. And though you are averse to my acquainting Lady Teazle with your passion, I'm sure she's not your enemy in the affair.

Jos. Surf. Pray, Sir Peter, now oblige me. I 10 am really too much affected by the subject we have been speaking of to bestow a thought on my own concerns. The man who is entrusted with his friend's distresses can never ——

Reënter SERVANT

Well, sir?   15

Ser. Your brother, sir, is speaking to a gentleman in the street, and says he knows you are within.

Jos. Surf. 'Sdeath, blockhead, I'm not within — I'm out for the day.

Sir Pet. Stay — hold — a thought has struck me: 20 — you shall be at home.

Jos. Surf. Well, well, let him come up. — [*Exit* SERVANT.] He'll interrupt Sir Peter, however.

[*Aside.*

Sir Pet. Now, my good friend, oblige me, I entreat you. Before Charles comes, let me conceal myself somewhere, then do you tax him on the point we have been talking, and his answer may satisfy
5 me at once.

Jos. Surf. Oh, fie, Sir Peter! would you have me join in so mean a trick? — to trepan my brother too?

Sir Pet. Nay, you tell me you are sure he is in-
10 nocent; if so, you do him the greatest service by giving him an opportunity to clear himself, and you will set my heart at rest. Come, you shall not refuse me: [*Going up,*] here, behind the screen will be — Hey! what the devil! there seems to be one
15 listener here already — I'll swear I saw a petticoat!

Jos. Surf. Ha! ha! ha! Well, this is ridiculous enough. I'll tell you, Sir Peter, though I hold a man of intrigue to be a most despicable character, yet, you know, it does not follow that one is to be an
20 absolute Joseph either! Hark'ee, 'tis a little French milliner, a silly rogue that plagues me; and having some character to lose, on your coming, sir, she ran behind the screen.

Sir Pet. Ah, Joseph! Joseph! Did I ever think
25 that you —— But, egad, she has overheard all I have been saying of my wife.

Jos. Surf. Oh, 'twill never go any farther, you may depend upon it!

Sir Pet. No! then, faith, let her hear it out. — Here's a closet will do as well.

Jos. Surf. Well, go in there.   5

Sir Pet. Sly rogue! sly rogue! [*Goes into the closet.*

Jos. Surf. A narrow escape, indeed! and a curious situation I'm in, to part man and wife in this manner.

Lady Teaz. [*Peeping.*] Couldn't I steal off?   10

Jos. Surf. Keep close, my angel!

Sir Pet. [*Peeping.*] Joseph, tax him home.

Jos. Surf. Back, my dear friend!

Lady Teaz. [*Peeping.*] Couldn't you lock Sir Peter in?   ,15

Jos. Surf. Be still, my life!

Sir Pet. [*Peeping.*] You're sure the little milliner won't blab?

Jos. Surf. In, in, my dear Sir Peter! — 'Fore Gad, I wish I had a key to the door.   20

Enter CHARLES SURFACE

Chas. Surf. Holla! brother, what has been the matter? Your fellow would not let me up at first. What! have you had a Jew with you?

Jos. Surf. No, brother, I assure you.

8

Chas. Surf. But what has made Sir Peter steal off? I thought he had been with you.

Jos. Surf. He was, brother; but, hearing you were coming, he did not choose to stay.

5 *Chas. Surf.* What! was the old gentleman afraid I wanted to borrow money of him?

Jos. Surf. No, sir: but I am sorry to find, Charles, you have lately given that worthy man grounds for great uneasiness.

10 *Chas. Surf.* Yes, they tell me I do that to a great many worthy men. But how so, pray?

Jos. Surf. To be plain with you, brother, he thinks you are endeavouring to gain Lady Teazle's affections from him.

15 *Chas. Surf.* Who, I? O Lud! not I, upon my word. — Ha! ha! ha! ha! so the old fellow has found out that he has got a young wife, has he? — or, what is worse, Lady Teazle has found out she has an old husband?

20 *Jos. Surf.* This is no subject to jest on, brother. He who can laugh ——

Chas. Surf. True, true, as you were going to say — then, seriously, I never had the least idea of what you charge me with, upon my honour.

25 *Jos. Surf.* Well, it will give Sir Peter great satisfaction to hear this.   [*Raising his voice.*

Chas. Surf. To be sure, I once thought the lady seemed to have taken a fancy to me; but, upon my soul, I never gave her the least encouragement. Besides, you know my attachment to Maria.   5

Jos. Surf. But sure, brother, even if Lady Teazle had betrayed the fondest partiality for you ——

Chas. Surf. Why, look'ee, Joseph, I hope I shall never deliberately do a dishonourable action; but if a pretty woman was purposely to throw herself 10 in my way — and that pretty woman married to a man old enough to be her father ——

Jos. Surf. Well!

Chas. Surf. Why, I believe I should be obliged to ——   15

Jos. Surf. What?

Chas. Surf. To borrow a little of your morality, that's all. But, brother, do you know now that you surprise me exceedingly, by naming me with Lady Teazle; for, i' faith, I always understood you were 20 her favourite.

Jos. Surf. Oh, for shame, Charles! This retort is foolish.

Chas. Surf. Nay, I swear I have seen you exchange such significant glances ——   25

Jos. Surf. Nay, nay, sir, this is no jest.

Chas. Surf. Egad, I'm serious! Don't you remember one day, when I called here ——

Jos. Surf. Nay, pr'ythee, Charles ——

Chas. Surf. And found you together ——

5   *Jos. Surf.* Zounds, sir, I insist ——

Chas. Surf. And another time when your servant ——

Jos. Surf. Brother, brother, a word with you! —
[*Aside.*] Gad, I must stop him.

10   *Chas. Surf.* Informed, I say, that ——

Jos. Surf. Hush! I beg your pardon, but Sir Peter
has overheard all we have been saying. I knew you
would clear yourself, or I should not have consented.

Chas. Surf. How, Sir Peter! Where is he?

15   *Jos. Surf.* Softly, there!   [*Points to the closet.*

Chas. Surf. Oh, 'fore Heaven, I'll have him out.
Sir Peter, come forth!

Jos. Surf. No, no ——

Chas. Surf. I say, Sir Peter, come into court. —

20 [*Pulls in* SIR PETER.] What! my old guardian! —
What! turn inquisitor, and take evidence incog.?
Oh, fie! Oh, fie!

Sir Pet. Give me your hand, Charles — I believe
I have suspected you wrongfully; but you mustn't

25 be angry with Joseph — 'twas my plan!

Chas. Surf. Indeed!

Sir Pet. But I acquit you. I promise you I don't think near so ill of you as I did: what I have heard has given me great satisfaction.

Chas. Surf. Egad, then, 'twas lucky you didn't hear any more. Wasn't it, Joseph?   5

Sir Pet. Ah! you would have retorted on him.

Chas. Surf. Ah, ay, that was a joke.

Sir Pet. Yes, yes, I know his honour too well.

Chas. Surf. But you might as well have suspected him as me in this matter, for all that.   Mightn't he, 10 Joseph?

Sir Pet. Well, well, I believe you.

Jos. Surf. Would they were both out of the room!
                                                    [*Aside.*

Sir Pet. And in future, perhaps, we may not be such strangers.   15

Reënter SERVANT, *and whispers* JOSEPH SURFACE

Ser. Lady Sneerwell is below, and says she will come up.

Jos. Surf. Lady Sneerwell!   Gad's life! she must not come here. [*Exit* SERVANT.]   Gentlemen, I beg pardon — I must wait on you down stairs: here is 20 a person come on particular business.

Chas. Surf. Well, you can see him in another

room. Sir Peter and I have not met a long time,
and I have something to say to him.

Jos. Surf. [*Aside.*] They must not be left together. — [*Aloud.*] I'll send Lady Sneerwell away,
5 and return directly. — [*Aside to* SIR PETER.] Sir
Peter, not a word of the French milliner.

Sir Pet. [*Aside to* JOSEPH SURFACE.] I! not for
the world! — [*Exit* JOSEPH SURFACE.] Ah, Charles,
if you associated more with your brother, one might
10 indeed hope for your reformation. He is a man of
sentiment. Well, there is nothing in the world so
noble as a man of sentiment.

Chas. Surf. Pshaw! he is too moral by half;
and so apprehensive· of his good name, as he calls
15 it.

Sir Pet. No, no, — come, come, — you wrong
him. No, no! Joseph is no rake, but he is no such
saint either, in that respect. — [*Aside.*] I have a
great mind to tell him — we should have such a laugh
20 at Joseph.

Chas. Surf. Oh, hang him! he's a very anchorite,
a young hermit!

Sir Pet. Hark'ee — you must not abuse him: he
may chance to hear of it again, I promise you.

25 *Chas. Surf.* Why, you won't tell him?

Sir Pet. No — but — this way. — [*Aside.*] Egad,

I'll tell him. — [*Aloud.*] Hark'ee — have you a
mind to have a good laugh at Joseph?
   Chas. Surf. I should like it of all things.
   Sir Pet. Then, i' faith, we will! I'll be quit with
him for discovering me. He had a girl with him 5
when I called.   [*Whispers.*
   Chas. Surf. What! Joseph? you jest.
   Sir Pet. Hush! — a little French milliner — and
the best of the jest is — she's in the room now.
   Chas. Surf. The devil she is!   10
   Sir Pet. Hush! I tell you. [*Points to the screen.*
   Chas. Surf. Behind the screen! 'Slife, let's un-
veil her!
   Sir Pet. No, no, he's coming: — you sha'n't, in-
deed!   15
   Chas. Surf. Oh, egad, we'll have a peep at the
little milliner!
   Sir Pet. Not for the world! — Joseph will never
forgive me.
   Chas. Surf. I'll stand by you ——   20
   Sir Pet. Odds, here he is!
        [CHARLES SURFACE *throws down the screen.*

           Reënter JOSEPH SURFACE

   Chas. Surf. Lady Teazle, by all that's wonderful.
   Sir Pet. Lady Teazle, by all that's damnable!

Chas. Surf. Sir Peter, this is one of the smartest
French milliners I ever saw. Egad, you seem all to
have been diverting yourselves here at hide and seek,
and I don't see who is out of the secret. Shall I
5 beg your ladyship to inform me? Not a word! —
Brother, will you be pleased to explain this matter?
What! is Morality dumb too? — Sir Peter, though
I found you in the dark, perhaps you are not so
now! All mute! — Well — though I can make noth-
10 ing of the affair, I suppose you perfectly understand
one another; so I'll leave you to yourselves. —
[*Going.*] Brother, I'm sorry to find you have given
that worthy man grounds for so much uneasiness.
— Sir Peter! there's nothing in the world so noble
15 as a man of sentiment!   [*Exit.*

Jos. Surf. Sir Peter — notwithstanding — I confess — that appearances are against me — if you
will afford me your patience — I make no doubt —
but I shall explain every thing to your satisfaction.
20 *Sir Pet.* If you please, sir.

Jos. Surf. The fact is, sir, that Lady Teazle,
knowing my pretensions to your ward Maria — I say,
sir, Lady Teazle, being apprehensive of the jealousy
of your temper — and knowing my friendship to
25 the family — she, sir, I say — called here — in
order that — I might explain these pretensions —

but on your coming — being apprehensive — as I said — of your jealousy — she withdrew — and this, you may depend on it, is the whole truth of the matter.

Sir Pet. A very clear account, upon my word; and I dare swear the lady will vouch for every article of it. 5

Lady Teaz. For not one word of it, Sir Peter!

Sir Pet. How! don't you think it worth while to agree in the lie?

Lady Teaz. There is not one syllable of truth in what that gentleman has told you.   10

Sir Pet. I believe you, upon my soul, ma'am!

Jos. Surf. [*Aside to* Lady Teazle.] 'Sdeath, madam, will you betray me?

Lady Teaz. Good Mr. Hypocrite, by your leave, I'll speak for myself.   15

Sir Pet. Ay, let her alone, sir; you'll find she'll make out a better story than you, without prompting.

Lady Teaz. Hear me, Sir Peter! — I came here on no matter relating to your ward, and even ig- 20 norant of this gentleman's pretensions to her. But I came, seduced by his insidious arguments, at least to listen to his pretended passion, if not to sacrifice your honour to his baseness.

Sir Pet. Now, I believe, the truth is coming, 25 indeed!

Jos. Surf. The woman's mad!

Lady Teaz. No, sir; she has recovered her senses, and your own arts have furnished her with the means. — Sir Peter, I do not expect you to credit
5 me — but the tenderness you expressed for me, when I am sure you could not think I was a witness to it, has so penetrated to my heart, that had I left the place without the shame of this discovery, my future life should have spoken the sincerity of my
10 gratitude. As for that smooth-tongued hypocrite, who would have seduced the wife of his too credulous friend, while he affected honourable addresses to his ward — I behold him now in a light so truly despicable, that I shall never again respect myself for hav-
15 ing listened to him.   [*Exit.*

Jos. Surf. Notwithstanding all this, Sir Peter, Heaven knows ——

Sir Pet. That you are a villain! and so I leave you to your conscience.

20 *Jos. Surf.* You are too rash, Sir Peter; you shall hear me. The man who shuts out conviction by refusing to ——

Sir Pet. Oh, damn your sentiments!

[*Exeunt* SIR PETER *and* JOSEPH SURFACE, *talking,*

ACT V

SCENE I. *The Library in Joseph Surface's House*

Enter JOSEPH SURFACE *and* SERVANT

Jos. Surf. Mr. Stanley! and why should you think I would see him? you must know he comes to ask something.

Ser. Sir, I should not have let him in, but that Mr. Rowley came to the door with him.   5

Jos. Surf. Pshaw! blockhead! to suppose that I should now be in a temper to receive visits from poor relations! — Well, why don't you show the fellow up?

Ser. I will, sir. — Why, sir, it was not my fault 10 that Sir Peter discovered my lady ——

Jos. Surf. Go, fool! — [*Exit* SERVANT.] Sure Fortune never played a man of my policy such a trick before! My character with Sir Peter, my hopes with Maria, destroyed in a moment! I'm in 15 a rare humour to listen to other people's distresses! I sha'n't be able to bestow even a benevolent senti- ment on Stanley. — So! here he comes, and Rowley with him. I must try to recover myself, and put a little charity into my face, however.   [*Exit.* 20

267

Enter SIR OLIVER SURFACE *and* ROWLEY

Sir Oliv. What! does he avoid us? That was
he, was it not?

Row. It was, sir. But I doubt you are come a
little too abruptly. His nerves are so weak, that
5 the sight of a poor relation may be too much for him.
I should have gone first to break it to him.

Sir Oliv. Oh, plague of his nerves! Yet this is
he whom Sir Peter extols as a man of the most
benevolent way of thinking!

10 *Row.* As to his way of thinking, I cannot pretend
to decide; for, to do him justice, he appears to have
as much speculative benevolence as any private
gentleman in the kingdom, though he is seldom
so sensual as to indulge himself in the exercise of
15 it.

Sir Oliv. Yet he has a string of charitable sentiments at his fingers' ends.

Row. Or, rather, at his tongue's end, Sir Oliver;
for I believe there is no sentiment he has such
20 faith in as that *Charity begins at home.*

Sir Oliv. And his, I presume, is of that domestic
sort which never stirs abroad at all.

Row. I doubt you'll find it so; but he's coming.
I mustn't seem to interrupt you; and you know, im-

mediately as you leave him, I come in to announce
your arrival in your real character.

Sir Oliv. True; and afterwards you'll meet me at
Sir Peter's.

Row. Without losing a moment.   [*Exit.* 5

Sir Oliv. I don't like the complaisance of his
features.

Reënter JOSEPH SURFACE

Jos. Surf. Sir, I beg you ten thousand pardons
for keeping you a moment waiting. — Mr. Stanley,
I presume.   10

Sir Oliv. At your service.

Jos. Surf. Sir, I beg you will do me the honour to
sit down — I entreat you, sir.

Sir Oliv. Dear sir — there's no occasion. —
[*Aside.*] Too civil by half!   15

Jos. Surf. I have not the pleasure of knowing
you, Mr. Stanley; but I am extremely happy to
see you look so well. You were nearly related to
my mother, I think, Mr. Stanley?

Sir Oliv. I was, sir; so nearly that my present 20
poverty, I fear, may do discredit to her wealthy chil-
dren, else I should not have presumed to trouble you.

Jos. Surf. Dear sir, there needs no apology; —
he that is in distress, though a stranger, has a right

to claim kindred with the wealthy. I am sure I wish I was one of that class, and had it in my power to offer you even a small relief.

Sir Oliv. If your uncle, Sir Oliver, were here, I
5 should have a friend.

Jos. Surf. I wish he was, sir, with all my heart: you should not want an advocate with him, believe me, sir.

Sir Oliv. I should not need one — my distresses
10 would recommend me. But I imagined his bounty would enable you to become the agent of his charity.

Jos. Surf. My dear sir, you were strangely misinformed. Sir Oliver is a worthy man, a very worthy man; but avarice, Mr. Stanley, is the vice of age.
15 I will tell you, my good sir, in confidence, what he has done for me has been a mere nothing; though people, I know, have thought otherwise, and for my part, I never chose to contradict the report.

Sir Oliv. What! has he never transmitted you
20 bullion — rupees — pagodas°?

Jos. Surf. Oh, dear sir, nothing of the kind! No, no; a few presents now and then — china, shawls, congo tea, avadavats° and Indian crackers -— little more, believe me.

25   *Sir Oliv.* Here's gratitude for twelve thousand pounds! — Avadavats and Indian crackers! [*Aside.*

Jos. Surf. Then, my dear sir, you have heard, I doubt not, of the extravagance of my brother: there are very few would credit what I have done for that unfortunate young man.

Sir Oliv. Not I, for one!   [*Aside.* 5

Jos. Surf. The sums I have lent him! Indeed I have been exceedingly to blame; it was an amiable weakness; however, I don't pretend to defend it — and now I feel it doubly culpable, since it has deprived me of the pleasure of serving you, Mr. Stan- 10 ley, as my heart dictates.

Sir Oliv. [*Aside.*] Dissembler! — [*Aloud.*] Then, sir, you can't assist me?

Jos. Surf. At present, it grieves me to say, I cannot; but, whenever I have the ability, you may 15 depend upon hearing from me.

Sir Oliv. I am extremely sorry ——

Jos. Surf. Not more than I, believe me; to pity, without the power to relieve, is still more painful than to ask and be denied.   20

Sir Oliv. Kind sir, your most obedient humble servant.

Jos. Surf. You leave me deeply affected, Mr. Stanley. — William, be ready to open the door.

[*Calls to* SERVANT.

Sir Oliv. Oh, dear sir, no ceremony.   25

Jos. Surf. Your very obedient.

Sir Oliv. Your most obsequious.

Jos. Surf. You may depend upon hearing from me, whenever I can be of service.

5 *Sir Oliv.* Sweet sir, you are too good!

Jos. Surf. In the meantime I wish you health and spirits.

Sir Oliv. Your ever grateful and perpetual humble servant.

10 *Jos. Surf.* Sir, yours as sincerely.

Sir Oliv. [*Aside.*] Now I am satisfied.   [*Exit.*

Jos. Surf. This is one bad effect of a good character; it invites application from the unfortunate, and there needs no small degree of address to gain 15 the reputation of benevolence without incurring the expense. The silver ore of pure charity is an expensive article in the catalogue of a man's good qualities; whereas the sentimental French plate I use instead of it makes just as good a show, and 20 pays no tax.

Reënter ROWLEY

Row. Mr. Surface, your servant: I was apprehensive of interrupting you, though my business demands immediate attention, as this note will inform you.

Jos. Surf. Always happy to see Mr. Rowley, —
a rascal. — [*Aside.* *Reads the letter.*] Sir Oliver
Surface! — My uncle arrived!

Row. He is, indeed: we have just parted —
quite well, after a speedy voyage, and impatient 5
to embrace his worthy nephew.

Jos. Surf. I am astonished! — William! stop Mr.
Stanley, if he's not gone.   [*Calls to* SERVANT.

Row. Oh! he's out of reach, I believe.

Jos. Surf. Why did you not let me know this 10
when you came in together?

Row. I thought you had particular business.
But I must be gone to inform your brother, and
appoint him here to meet your uncle. He will
be with you in a quarter of an hour.   15

Jos. Surf. So he says. Well, I am strangely
overjoyed at his coming. — [*Aside.*] Never, to be
sure, was any thing so unlucky!

Row. You will be delighted to see how well he
looks.   20

Jos. Surf. Oh! I'm overjoyed to hear it. —
[*Aside.*] Just at this time!

Row. I'll tell him how impatiently you expect
him.

Jos. Surf. Do, do; pray give my best duty and 25
affection. Indeed, I cannot express the sensa-

T

tions I feel at the thought of seeing him. — [*Exit*
ROWLEY.] Certainly his coming just at this time
is the cruellest piece of ill fortune.   [*Exit.*

SCENE II. *A Room in Sir Peter Teazle's House*

Enter MRS. CANDOUR *and* MAID

Maid. Indeed, ma'am, my lady will see nobody
5 at present.
Mrs. Can. Did you tell her it was her friend
Mrs. Candour?
Maid. Yes, ma'am; but she begs you will excuse
her.
10 *Mrs. Can.* Do go again; I shall be glad to see
her, if it be only for a moment, for I am sure she
must be in great distress. — [*Exit* MAID.] Dear
heart, how provoking! I'm not mistress of half
the circumstances! We shall have the whole affair
15 in the newspapers, with the names of the parties
at length, before I have dropped the story at a
dozen houses.

Enter SIR BENJAMIN BACKBITE

Oh, dear Sir Benjamin! you have heard, I suppose ——
20 *Sir Ben.* Of Lady Teazle and Mr. Surface ——

Mrs. Can. And Sir Peter's discovery ——

Sir Ben. Oh, the strangest piece of business, to be sure!

Mrs. Can. Well, I never was so surprised in my life. I am so sorry for all parties, indeed. 5

Sir Ben. Now, I don't pity Sir Peter at all: he was so extravagantly partial to Mr. Surface.

Mrs. Can. Mr. Surface! Why, 'twas with Charles Lady Teazle was detected.

Sir Ben. No, no, I tell you: Mr. Surface is the 10 gallant.

Mrs. Can. No such thing! Charles is the man. 'Twas Mr. Surface brought Sir Peter on purpose to discover them.

Sir Ben. I tell you I had it from one —— 15

Mrs. Can. And I have it from one ——

Sir Ben. Who had it from one, who had it ——

Mrs. Can. From one immediately. But here comes Lady Sneerwell; perhaps she knows the whole affair. 20

Enter LADY SNEERWELL

Lady Sneer. So, my dear Mrs. Candour, here's a sad affair of our friend Lady Teazle!

Mrs. Can. Ay, my dear friend, who would have thought ——

Lady Sneer. Well, there is no trusting appearances; though, indeed, she was always too lively for me.

Mrs. Can. To be sure, her manners were a little 5 too free; but then she was so young!

Lady Sneer. And had, indeed, some good qualities.

Mrs. Can. So she had, indeed. But have you heard the particulars?

10 *Lady Sneer.* No; but every body says that Mr. Surface ——

Sir Ben. Ay, there; I told you Mr. Surface was the man.

Mrs. Can. No, no: indeed it was Charles.

15 *Lady Sneer.* Charles! You alarm me, Mrs. Candour!

Mrs. Can. Yes, yes; he was the lover. Mr. Surface, to do him justice, was only the informer.

Sir Ben. Well, I'll not dispute with you, Mrs. 20 Candour; but, be it which it may, I hope that Sir Peter's wound will not ——

Mrs. Can. Sir Peter's wound! Oh, mercy! I didn't hear a word of their fighting.

Lady Sneer. Nor I, a syllable.

25 *Sir Ben.* No! what, no mention of the duel?

Mrs. Can. Not a word.

Sir Ben. Oh, yes: they fought before they left the room.

Lady Sneer. Pray, let us hear.

Mrs. Can. Ay, do oblige us with the duel.

Sir Ben. Sir, says Sir Peter, immediately after 5 the discovery, *you are a most ungrateful fellow.*

Mrs. Can. Ay, to Charles ——

Sir Ben. No, no — to Mr. Surface — *a most ungrateful fellow; and old as I am, sir*, says he, *I insist on immediate satisfaction.* 10

Mrs. Can. Ay, that must have been to Charles; for 'tis very unlikely Mr. Surface should fight in his own house.

Sir Ben. Gad's life, ma'am, not at all — *giving me immediate satisfaction.* — On this, ma'am, Lady 15 Teazle, seeing Sir Peter in such danger, ran out of the room in strong hysterics, and Charles after her, calling out for hartshorn° and water; then, madam, they began to fight with swords ——

Enter CRABTREE

Crab. With pistols, nephew, pistols! I have it 20 from undoubted authority.

Mrs. Can. Oh, Mr. Crabtree, then it is all true!

Crab. Too true, indeed, madam, and Sir Peter is dangerously wounded ——

Sir Ben. By a thrust in segoon° quite through
his left side ——

Crab. By a bullet lodged in the thorax.

Mrs. Can. Mercy on me! Poor Sir Peter!

5 *Crab.* Yes, madam; though Charles would have
avoided the matter, if he could.

Mrs. Can. I told you who it was; I knew Charles
was the person.

Sir Ben. My uncle, I see, knows nothing of
10 the matter.

Crab. But Sir Peter taxed him with the basest
ingratitude ——

Sir Ben. That I told you, you know ——

Crab. Do, nephew, let me speak! — and in-
15 sisted on immediate ——

Sir Ben. Just as I said ——

Crab. Odds life, nephew, allow others to know
something too! A pair of pistols lay on the bureau
(for Mr. Surface, it seems, had come home the night
20 before late from Salthill,° where he had been to
see the Montem° with a friend, who has a son at
Eton), so, unluckily, the pistols were left charged.

Sir Ben. I heard nothing of this.

Crab. Sir Peter forced Charles to take one,
25 and they fired, it seems, pretty nearly together.
Charles's shot took effect, as I tell you, and Sir

Peter's missed; but, what is very extraordinary, the ball struck against a little bronze Shakespeare that stood over the fire-place, grazed out of the window at a right angle, and wounded the post-man, who was just coming to the door with a double 5 letter from Northamptonshire.

Sir Ben. My uncle's account is more circum-stantial, I confess; but I believe mine is the true one, for all that.

Lady Sneer. [*Aside.*] I am more interested in 10 this affair than they imagine, and must have better information.   [*Exit.*

Sir Ben. Ah! Lady Sneerwell's alarm is very easily accounted for.

Crab. Yes, yes, they certainly do say — but 15 that's neither here nor there.

Mrs. Can. But, pray, where is Sir Peter at present?

Crab. Oh! they brought him home, and he is now in the house, though the servants are ordered 20 to deny him.

Mrs. Can. I believe so, and Lady Teazle, I sup-pose, attending him.

Crab. Yes, yes; and I saw one of the faculty enter just before me.   25

Sir Ben. Hey! who comes here?

Crab. Oh, this is he: the physician, depend on't.

Mrs. Can. Oh, certainly! it must be the physician; and now we shall know.

Enter SIR OLIVER SURFACE

Crab. Well, doctor, what hopes?

5 *Mrs. Can.* Ay, doctor, how's your patient?

Sir Ben. Now, doctor, isn't it a wound with a small-sword?

Crab. A bullet lodged in the thorax, for a hundred!

10 *Sir Oliv.* Doctor! a wound with a small-sword! and a bullet in the thorax! — Oons! are you mad, good people?

Sir Ben. Perhaps, sir, you are not a doctor?

Sir Oliv. Truly, I am to thank you for my degree, 15 if I am.

Crab. Only a friend of Sir Peter's, then, I presume. But, sir, you must have heard of his accident?

Sir Oliv. Not a word!

20 *Crab.* Not of his being dangerously wounded?

Sir Oliv. The devil he is!

Sir Ben. Run through the body ——

Crab. Shot in the breast ——

Sir Ben. By one Mr. Surface ——

Crab. Ay, the younger.

Sir Oliv. Hey! what the plague! you seem to differ strangely in your accounts: however, you agree that Sir Peter is dangerously wounded.

Sir Ben. Oh, yes, we agree in that.   5

Crab. Yes, yes, I believe there can be no doubt of that.

Sir Oliv. Then, upon my word, for a person in that situation, he is the most imprudent man alive; for here he comes, walking as if nothing at all was 10 the matter.

Enter Sir Peter Teazle

Odds heart, Sir Peter! you are come in good time, I promise you; for we had just given you over!

Sir Ben. [*Aside to* Crabtree.] Egad, uncle, this is the most sudden recovery!   15

Sir Oliv. Why, man! what do you out of bed with a small-sword through your body, and a bullet lodged in your thorax?

Sir Pet. A small-sword and a bullet!

Sir Oliv. Ay; these gentlemen would have 20 killed you without law or physic, and wanted to dub me a doctor, to make me an accomplice.

Sir Pet. Why, what is all this?

Sir Ben. We rejoice, Sir Peter, that the story

of the duel is not true, and are sincerely sorry for
your other misfortune.

Sir Pet. So, so; all over the town already!

[*Aside.*

Crab. Though, Sir Peter, you were certainly vastly
5 to blame to marry at your years.

Sir Pet. Sir, what business is that of yours?

Mrs. Can. Though, indeed, as Sir Peter made
so good a husband, he's very much to be pitied.

Sir Pet. Plague on your pity, ma'am! I desire
10 none of it.

Sir Ben. However, Sir Peter, you must not mind
the laughing and jests you will meet with on the
occasion.

Sir Pet. Sir, sir! I desire to be master in my
15 own house.

Crab. 'Tis no uncommon case, that's one comfort.

Sir Pet. I insist on being left to myself: without ceremony, I insist on your leaving my house
20 directly!

Mrs. Can. Well, well, we are going; and depend
on't, we'll make the best report of it we can.   [*Exit.*

Sir Pet. Leave my house!

Crab. And tell how hardly you've been treated.

[*Exit.*

Sir Pet. Leave my house!

Sir Ben. And how patiently you bear it. [*Exit.*

Sir Pet. Fiends! vipers! furies! Oh! that their own venom would choke them!

Sir Oliv. They are very provoking indeed, Sir 5 Peter.

Enter ROWLEY

Row. I heard high words: what has ruffled you, sir?

Sir Pet. Pshaw! what signifies asking? Do I ever pass a day without my vexations? 10

Row. Well, I'm not inquisitive.

Sir Oliv. Well, Sir Peter, I have seen both my nephews in the manner we proposed.

Sir Pet. A precious couple they are!

Row. Yes, and Sir Oliver is convinced that your 15 judgment was right, Sir Peter.

Sir Oliv. Yes, I find Joseph is indeed the man, after all.

Row. Ay, as Sir Peter says, he is a man of sentiment. 20

Sir Oliv. And acts up to the sentiments he professes.

Row. It certainly is edification to hear him talk.

Sir Oliv. Oh, he's a model for the young men of

the age! — but how's this, Sir Peter? you don't
join us in your friend Joseph's praise, as I expected.

Sir Pet. Sir Oliver, we live in a wicked world,
and the fewer we praise the better.

5   *Row.* What! do you say so, Sir Peter, who
were never mistaken in your life?

Sir Pet. Pshaw! plague on you both! I see by
your sneering you have heard the whole affair. I
shall go mad among you!

10   *Row.* Then, to fret you no longer, Sir Peter, we
are indeed acquainted with it all. I met Lady
Teazle coming from Mr. Surface's so humbled,
that she deigned to request me to be her advocate
with you.

15   *Sir Pet.* And does Sir Oliver know all this?

Sir Oliv. Every circumstance.

Sir Pet. What, of the closet and the screen, hey?

Sir Oliv. Yes, yes, and the little French milliner.
Oh, I have been vastly diverted with the story!
20 ha! ha! ha!

Sir Pet. 'Twas very pleasant.

Sir Oliv. I never laughed more in my life, I
assure you: ah! ah! ah!

Sir Pet. Oh, vastly diverting! ha! ha! ha!

25   *Row.* To be sure, Joseph with his sentiments!
ha! ha! ha!

Sir Pet. Yes, yes, his sentiments! ha! ha! ha! Hypocritical villain!

Sir Oliv. Ay, and that rogue Charles to pull Sir Peter out of the closet: ha! ha! ha!

Sir Pet. Ha! ha! 'twas devilish entertaining, 5 to be sure!

Sir Oliv. Ha! ha! ha! Egad, Sir Peter, I should like to have seen your face when the screen was thrown down: ha! ha!

Sir Pet. Yes, yes, my face when the screen was 10 thrown down: ha! ha! ha! Oh, I must never show my head again!

Sir Oliv. But come, come, it isn't fair to laugh at you neither, my old friend; though, upon my soul, I can't help it. 15

Sir Pet. Oh, pray don't restrain your mirth on my account: it does not hurt me at all! I laugh at the whole affair myself. Yes, yes, I think being a standing jest for all one's acquaintance a very happy situation. Oh, yes, and then of a morning 20 to read the paragraphs about Mr. S——, Lady T——, and Sir P——, will be so entertaining!

Row. Without affectation, Sir Peter, you may despise the ridicule of fools. But I see Lady Teazle going towards the next room; I am sure you must 25 desire a reconciliation as earnestly as she does.

Sir Oliv. Perhaps my being here prevents her coming to you. Well, I'll leave honest Rowley to mediate between you; but he must bring you all presently to Mr. Surface's, where I am now
5 returning, if not to reclaim a libertine, at least to expose hypocrisy.

Sir Pet. Ah, I'll be present at your discovering yourself there with all my heart; though 'tis a vile unlucky place for discoveries.

10 *Row.* We'll follow. [*Exit* SIR OLIVER SURFACE.

Sir Pet. She is not coming here, you see, Rowley.

Row. No, but she has left the door of that room open, you perceive. See, she is in tears.

Sir Pet. Certainly a little mortification appears
15 very becoming in a wife. Don't you think it will do her good to let her pine a little?

Row. Oh, this is ungenerous in you!

Sir Pet. Well, I know not what to think. You remember the letter I found of hers evidently in-
20 tended for Charles?

Row. A mere forgery, Sir Peter! laid in your way on purpose. This is one of the points which I intend Snake shall give you conviction of.

Sir Pet. I wish I were once satisfied of that. She
25 looks this way. What a remarkably elegant turn of the head she has! Rowley, I'll go to her.

Row. Certainly.

Sir Pet. Though, when it is known that we are reconciled, people will laugh at me ten times more.

Row. Let them laugh, and retort their malice only by showing them you are happy in spite of it. 5

Sir Pet. I' faith, so I will! and, if I'm not mistaken, we may yet be the happiest couple in the country.

Row. Nay, Sir Peter, he who once lays aside suspicion —— 10

Sir Pet. Hold, Master Rowley! if you have any regard for me, never let me hear you utter any thing like a sentiment: I have had enough of them to serve me the rest of my life.   [*Exeunt.*

SCENE III.   *The Library in Joseph Surface's House*

Enter JOSEPH SURFACE *and* LADY SNEERWELL

Lady Sneer. Impossible! Will not Sir Peter im- 15 mediately be reconciled to Charles, and of course no longer oppose his union with Maria? The thought is distraction to me.

Jos. Surf. Can passion furnish a remedy?

Lady Sneer. No, nor cunning either. Oh, I was 20 a fool, an idiot, to league with such a blunderer!

Jos. Surf. Sure, Lady Sneerwell, I am the greatest
sufferer; yet you see I bear the accident with calm-
ness.

Lady Sneer. Because the disappointment doesn't
5 reach your heart; your interest only attached you
to Maria. Had you felt for her what I have for
that ungrateful libertine, neither your temper nor
hypocrisy could prevent your showing the sharpness
of your vexation.

10 *Jos. Surf.* But why should your reproaches fall
on me for this disappointment?

Lady Sneer. Are you not the cause of it? Had
you not a sufficient field for your roguery in im-
posing upon Sir Peter, and supplanting your brother,
15 but you must endeavour to seduce his wife? I hate
such an avarice of crimes; 'tis an unfair monopoly,
and never prospers.

Jos. Surf. Well, I admit I have been to blame.
I confess I deviated from the direct road of wrong,
20 but I don't think we're so totally defeated neither.

Lady Sneer. No!

Jos. Surf. You tell me you have made a trial
of Snake since we met, and that you still believe
him faithful to us?

25 *Lady Sneer.* I do believe so.

Jos. Surf. And that he has undertaken, should it

be necessary, to swear and prove, that Charles is at
this time contracted by vows and honour to your
ladyship, which some of his former letters to you
will serve to support?

Lady Sneer. This, indeed, might have assisted.   5

Jos. Surf. Come, come; it is not too late yet. —
[*Knocking at the door.*]   But hark! this is probably
my uncle, Sir Oliver: retire to that room; we'll
consult farther when he is gone.

Lady Sneer. Well, but if he should find you out 10
too?

Jos. Surf. Oh, I have no fear of that. Sir Peter
will hold his tongue for his own credit's sake — and
you may depend on it I shall soon discover Sir
Oliver's weak side!   15

Lady Sneer. I have no diffidence of your abili- .
ties: only be constant to one roguery at a time.

Jos. Surf. I will, I will! — [*Exit* LADY SNEER-
WELL.] So! 'tis confounded hard, after such bad
fortune, to be baited by one's confederate in evil. 20
Well, at all events, my character is so much better
than Charles's, that I certainly — hey! — what —
this is not Sir Oliver, but old Stanley again. Plague
on't that he should return to tease me just now!
I shall have Sir Oliver come and find him here — 25
and ——

U

Enter Sir Oliver Surface

Gad's life, Mr. Stanley, why have you come back to plague me at this time? You must not stay now, upon my word.

Sir Oliv. Sir, I hear your uncle Oliver is expected
5 here, and though he has been so penurious to you, I'll try what he'll do for me.

Jos. Surf. Sir, 'tis impossible for you to stay now, so I must beg —— Come any other time, and I promise you, you shall be assisted.

10   *Sir Oliv.* No: Sir Oliver and I must be acquainted.

Jos. Surf. Zounds, sir! then I insist on your quitting the room directly.

Sir Oliv. Nay, sir ——

Jos. Surf. Sir, I insist on't! — Here, William!
15 show this gentleman out. Since you compel me, sir, not one moment — this is such insolence.

[Going to push him out.

Enter Charles Surface

Chas. Surf. Heyday! what's the matter now? What the devil, have you got hold of my little broker here? Zounds, brother, don't hurt little
20 Premium. What's the matter, my little fellow?

Jos. Surf. So! he has been with you too, has he?

Chas. Surf. To be sure, he has. Why, he's as honest a little —— But sure, Joseph, you have not been borrowing money too, have you?

Jos. Surf. Borrowing! no! But, brother, you know we expect Sir Oliver here every ——   5

Chas. Surf. O Gad, that's true! Noll mustn't find the little broker here, to be sure.

Jos. Surf. Yet Mr. Stanley insists ——

Chas. Surf. Stanley! why his name's Premium.

Jos. Surf. No, sir, Stanley.   10

Chas. Surf. No, no, Premium.

Jos. Surf. Well, no matter which — but ——

Chas. Surf. Ay, ay, Stanley or Premium, 'tis the same thing, as you say; for I suppose he goes by half a hundred names, besides A. B. at the coffee-   15
house.°   [*Knocking.*

Jos. Surf. 'Sdeath! here's Sir Oliver at the door. — Now I beg, Mr. Stanley ——

Chas. Surf. Ay, ay, and I beg, Mr. Premium ——

Sir Oliv. Gentlemen ——   20

Jos. Surf. Sir, by Heaven you shall go!

Chas. Surf. Ay, out with him, certainly!

Sir Oliv. This violence ——

Jos. Surf. Sir, 'tis your own fault.

Chas. Surf. Out with him, to be sure.   25

[*Both forcing* Sir Oliver *out.*

Enter SIR PETER *and* LADY TEAZLE, MARIA, *and*
ROWLEY

Sir Pet. My old friend, Sir Oliver — hey! What
in the name of wonder — here are dutiful nephews
— assault their uncle at a first visit!

Lady Teaz. Indeed, Sir Oliver, 'twas well we came
5 in to rescue you.

Row. Truly it was; for I perceive, Sir Oliver, the
character of old Stanley was no protection to you.

Sir Oliv. Nor of Premium either: the necessities
of the former could not extort a shilling from that
10 benevolent gentleman; and with the other I stood
a chance of faring worse than my ancestors, and
being knocked down without being bid for.

Jos. Surf. Charles!

Chas. Surf. Joseph!

15 *Jos. Surf.* 'Tis now complete!

Chas. Surf. Very.

Sir Oliv. Sir Peter, my friend, and Rowley too —
look on that elder nephew of mine. You know
what he has already received from my bounty;
20 and you also know how gladly I would have regarded
half my fortune as held in trust for him: judge
then my disappointment in discovering him to be
destitute of truth, charity, and gratitude!

Sir Pet. Sir Oliver, I should be more surprised at this declaration, if I had not myself found him to be mean, treacherous, and hypocritical.

Lady Teaz. And if the gentleman pleads not guilty to these, pray let him call me to his character. ₅

Sir Pet. Then, I believe, we need add no more: if he knows himself, he will consider it as the most perfect punishment, that he is known to the world.

Chas. Surf. If they talk this way to Honesty, what will they say to me, by and by?   [*Aside.* ₁₀

[Sir Peter, Lady Teazle, *and* Maria *retire.*

Sir Oliv. As for that prodigal, his brother, there ——

Chas. Surf. Ay, now comes my turn: the family pictures will ruin me!   [*Aside.*

Jos. Surf. Sir Oliver — uncle, will you honour ₁₅ me with a hearing?

Chas. Surf. Now, if Joseph would make one of his long speeches, I might recollect myself a little.
[*Aside.*

Sir Oliv. [*To* Joseph Surface.]   I suppose you would undertake to justify yourself?   ₂₀

Jos. Surf. I trust I could.

Sir Oliv. [*To* Charles Surface.] Well, sir! — and you could justify yourself too, I suppose?

Chas. Surf. Not that I know of, Sir Oliver.

Sir Oliv. What! — Little Premium has been let too much into the secret, I suppose?

Chas. Surf. True, sir; but they were family secrets, and should not be mentioned again, you know.

5 *Row.* Come, Sir Oliver, I know you cannot speak of Charles's follies with anger.

Sir Oliv. Odds heart, no more I can; nor with gravity either. Sir Peter, do you know the rogue bargained with me for all his ancestors; sold me 10 judges and generals by the foot, and maiden aunts as cheap as broken china.

Chas. Surf. To be sure, Sir Oliver, I did make a little free with the family canvas, that's the truth on't. My ancestors may rise in judgment against 15 me, there's no denying it; but believe me sincere when I tell you — and upon my soul I would not say so if I was not — that if I do not appear mortified at the exposure of my follies, it is because I feel at this moment the warmest satisfaction in seeing you, 20 my liberal benefactor.

Sir Oliv. Charles, I believe you. Give me your hand again: the ill-looking little fellow over the settee has made your peace.

Chas. Surf. Then, sir, my gratitude to the original 25 is still increased.

Lady Teaz. [*Advancing.*] Yet, I believe, Sir Oli-

ver, here is one whom Charles is still more anxious
to be reconciled to.   [*Pointing to* MARIA.

Sir Oliv. Oh, I have heard of his attachment
there; and, with the young lady's pardon, if I con-
strue right — that blush ——   5

Sir Pet. Well, child, speak your sentiments!

Mar. Sir, I have little to say, but that I shall
rejoice to hear that he is happy; for me, whatever
claim I had to his attention, I willingly resign to
one who has a better title.   10

Chas. Surf. How, Maria!

Sir Pet. Heyday! what's the mystery now?
While he appeared an incorrigible rake, you would
give your hand to no one else; and now that he is
likely to reform I'll warrant you won't have him!   15

Mar. His own heart and Lady Sneerwell know
the cause.

Chas. Surf. Lady Sneerwell!

Jos. Surf. Brother, it is with great concern I am
obliged to speak on this point, but my regard to   20
justice compels me, and Lady Sneerwell's injuries
can no longer be concealed.   [*Opens the door.*

Enter LADY SNEERWELL

Sir Pet. So! another French milliner! Egad, he
has one in every room in the house, I suppose!

Lady Sneer. Ungrateful Charles! Well may you be surprised, and feel for the indelicate situation your perfidy has forced me into.

Chas. Surf. Pray, uncle, is this another plot
5 of yours? For, as I have life, I don't understand it.

Jos. Surf. I believe, sir, there is but the evidence of one person more necessary to make it extremely clear.

10 *Sir Pet.* And that person, I imagine, is Mr. Snake. — Rowley, you were perfectly right to bring him with us, and pray let him appear.

Row. Walk in, Mr. Snake.

Enter SNAKE

I thought his testimony might be wanted: how-
15 ever, it happens unluckily, that he comes to confront Lady Sneerwell, not to support her.

Lady Sneer. A villain! Treacherous to me at last! Speak, fellow, have you too conspired against me!

20 *Snake.* I beg your ladyship ten thousand pardons: you paid me extremely liberally for the lie in question; but I unfortunately have been offered double to speak the truth.

Sir Pet. Plot and counter-plot, egad!

Lady Sneer. The torments of shame and disappointment on you all!   [*Going.*

Lady Teaz. Hold, Lady Sneerwell — before you go, let me thank you for the trouble you and that 5 gentleman have taken, in writing letters from me to Charles, and answering them yourself; and let me also request you to make my respects to the scandalous college, of which you are president, and inform them, that Lady Teazle, licentiate,° begs 10 leave to return the diploma they granted her, as she leaves off practice, and kills characters no longer.

Lady Sneer. You too, madam! — provoking — insolent! May your husband live these fifty years! 15
                                        [*Exit.*

Sir Pet. Oons! what a fury!

Lady Teaz. A malicious creature, indeed!

Sir Pet. What! not for her last wish?

Lady Teaz. Oh, no!

Sir Oliv. Well, sir, and what have you to say now? 20

Jos. Surf. Sir, I am so confounded, to find that Lady Sneerwell could be guilty of suborning Mr. Snake in this manner, to impose on us all, that I know not what to say: however, lest her revengeful spirit should prompt her to injure my brother, I 25

had certainly better follow her directly. For the
man who attempts to ——   [*Exit.*

Sir Pet. Moral to the last!

Sir Oliv. Ay, and marry her, Joseph, if you can.
5 Oil and vinegar! — egad you'll do very well together.

Row. I believe we have no more occasion for
Mr. Snake at present?

Snake. Before I go, I beg pardon once for all,
10 for whatever uneasiness I have been the humble
instrument of causing to the parties present.

 . *Sir Pet.* Well, well, you have made atonement
by a good deed at last.

Snake. But I must request of the company, that
15 it shall never be known.

Sir Pet. Hey! what the plague! are you ashamed
of having done a right thing once in your life?

Snake. Ah, sir, consider — I live by the badness
of my character; and, if it were once known that
20 I had been betrayed into an honest action, I should
lose every friend I have in the world.

Sir Oliv. Well, well — we'll not traduce you by
saying any thing in your praise, never fear.

     [*Exit* SNAKE.

Sir Pet. There's a precious rogue!

25 *Lady Teaz.* See, Sir Oliver, there needs no

persuasion now to reconcile your nephew and
Maria.

Sir Oliv. Ay, ay, that's as it should be, and, egad,
we'll have the wedding to-morrow morning.

Chas. Surf. Thank you, dear uncle.   5

Sir Pet. What, you rogue! don't you ask the
girl's consent first?

Chas. Surf. Oh, I have done that a long time —
a minute ago — and she has looked yes.

Mar. For shame, Charles! — I protest, Sir Peter, 10
there has not been a word ——

Sir Oliv. Well, then, the fewer the better; may
your love for each other never know abatement.

Sir Pet. And may you live as happily together as
Lady Teazle and I intend to do!   15

Chas. Surf. Rowley, my old friend, I am sure
you congratulate me; and I suspect that I owe you
much.

Sir Oliv. You do, indeed, Charles.

Sir Pet. Ay, honest Rowley always said you 20
would reform.

Chas. Surf. Why, as to reforming, Sir Peter, I'll
make no promises, and that I take to be a proof that
I intend to set about it. But here shall be my
monitor — my gentle guide. — Ah! can I leave the 25
virtuous path those eyes illumine?

Though thou, dear maid, shouldst waive thy
     beauty's sway,
Thou still must rule, because I will obey:
An humble fugitive from Folly view,
No sanctuary near but Love and you:

                         [*To the audience.*

5 You can, indeed, each anxious fear remove,
   For even Scandal dies, if you approve.

                           [*Exeunt omnes.*

EPILOGUE

BY MR. COLMAN°

SPOKEN BY LADY TEAZLE

I, who was late so volatile and gay,
Like a trade-wind must now blow all one way,
Bend all my cares, my studies, and my vows,
To one dull rusty weathercock — my spouse!
So wills our virtuous bard — the motley Bayes°   5
Of crying epilogues and laughing plays!
Old bachelors, who marry smart young wives,
Learn from our play to regulate your lives:
Each bring his dear to town, all faults upon her —
London will prove the very source of honour.   10
Plunged fairly in, like a cold bath it serves,
When principles relax, to brace the nerves:
Such is my case; and yet I must deplore
That the gay dream of dissipation's o'er.
And say, ye fair! was ever lively wife,   15
Born with a genius for the highest life,
Like me untimely blasted in her bloom,
Like me condemn'd to such a dismal doom?
Save money — when I just knew how to waste it!
Leave London — just as I began to taste it!   20

301

Must I then watch the early crowing cock,
The melancholy ticking of a clock;
In a lone rustic hall for ever pounded,
With dogs, cats, rats, and squalling brats sur-
    rounded.
5 With humble curaté can I now retire,
(While good Sir Peter boozes with the squire,)
And at backgammon mortify my soul,
That pants for loo, or flutters at a vole°?
Seven's the main°! Dear sound that must expire,
10 Lost at hot cockles round a Christmas fire;
The transient hour of fashion too soon spent,
Farewell the tranquil mind, farewell content!
Farewell the plumèd head, the cushioned tête,
That takes the cushion from its proper seat!
15 That spirit-stirring drum! — card drums I mean,
Spadille — odd   trick — pam — basto — king   and
    queen°!
And you, ye knockers, that, with brazen throat,
The welcome visitors' approach denote;
Farewell all quality of high renown,
20 Pride, pomp, and circumstance of glorious town!
Farewell! your revels I partake no more,
And Lady Teazle's occupation's o'er!
All this I told our bard; he smiled, and said 'twas
    clear,

I ought to play deep tragedy next year.
Meanwhile he drew wise morals from his play,
And in these solemn periods stalked away: —
"Blessed were the fair like you; her faults who
    stopped
And closed her follies when the curtain dropped!   5
No more in vice or error to engage,
Or play the fool at large on life's great stage."

NOTES

THE RIVALS

Withdrawing of the piece. See Introduction.

Mr. Harris, proprietor and manager of the Covent Garden Theatre.

Covent Garden Theatre, built in 1731 by John Rich, has been the scene of many first night plays. Garrick, Kemble, and other famous actors have played there.

2 : 3. Sons of Phœbus. Phœbus, another name for Apollo, god of poetry, hence poets.

2 : 4. The Fleet. A prison nearly eight hundred years old when it was destroyed in 1846. As early as 1290 it became a debtors' prison, for which purpose it was entirely reserved after 1641.

2 : 6. Sprig of bays. Bay, berry, especially of the laurel, hence a garland or crown bestowed as a prize for excellence, usually literary excellence.

2 : 23.. Drury Lane Theatre was one of the principal theatres of London. It was opened in 1663, rebuilt in 1674 by Sir Christopher Wren, and reopened in 1794 and 1812. Many of the great actors of the eighteenth and nineteenth centuries have played in this theatre.

6 : 3. Odd's life. A large variety of oaths in this play.

" Odd's life," a corruption of *God's life;* " Zounds " or "Oons," *God's wounds*. Of the same nature are "'Sdeath," "'Sblood," " Zooks," " odds jigs and tabors," " odds flints, pans, and triggers," " odds triggers and flints," " odds whips and wheels," " odds crickets," " odds swimmings," " odds frogs and tambours," " odds rabbit it," many of which are perfectly meaningless.

8 : 17. **Zounds**, see above.

8 : 21. **Thread papers**. Strips of paper for rolling up skeins of thread.

8 : 23. **Set of thousands**. " A team of six horses worth thousands of pounds."

9 : 8. **Mort o' merry-making**. *Mort* means much, or a great quantity.

9 : 12. **Pump room**. The room connected with the mineral springs, where the waters are drunk.

9 : 24. **Wig**. After the reign of Louis XIII., in France the wig became a distinctive feature of costume. " For more than a century no gentleman of fashion could appear without one. Such was the extravagance in this article of dress that as much as three guineas an ounce was paid in England for fine qualities of hair, and wigs were made at the cost of £140. It was only toward the end of the eighteenth century that the unnaturalness of this ornament seems to have been thought of and it began to be superseded by the queue with hair powder."

9 : 26. **Ton** = style.

10 : 14. .**Thoff** = though. **Jack Gauge**. Gauger, officer who measures contents of casks.

10 : 15. **Ta'en to his carrots.** Has taken to his natural hair, which happened to be the color of carrots.

10 : 16. **Bob.** A kind of wig. See *Century Dictionary.*

10 : 20. **Zooks.** Contraction of *Godzooks.* "Apparently a corruption of *God's* (that is, Christ's) *hooks*, with reference to the nails with which Christ was fixed on the Cross." — *Century Dictionary.*

11 : 2. **Gyde's porch.** "The lower rooms on the walks kept by Mr. Gyde, had, from their situation, some advantages, particularly a good garden and a retired walk on the margin of the river." (*The New Prose Bath Guide*, 1778; note by Aitken, Temple edition of *The Rivals.*)

11 : 6. **Circulating library.** For a complete account of the books mentioned in this play, see Nettleton's Introduction to his edition of *The Major Dramas of Sheridan,* lxviii–lxxvii.

12 : 19. **Blonds.** "Silk lace of two threads, twisted and formed in hexagonal meshes." — *Oxford Dictionary.*

12 : 20. **Sal volatile.** "The horns of the hart and ox were formerly much used as a source of ammonia, and the products of the distillation were employed in medicine under the name of sal volatile, volatile salt, hartshorn, or spirit of hartshorn." — *Century Dictionary.*

14 : 3. **Rout.** Large social gathering.

18 : 12. **Lud.** Corruption of *Lord.*

18 : 14. **Coz.** Contraction of *cousin*, used often familiarly when no such relationship exists.

19 : 19. **Illiterate**, obliterate.

20 : 13. **Extirpate**, exculpate.

20 : 15. **Controvertible**, incontrovertible.

21 : 15. **Intricate**, obstinate (?).

21 : 20. **Black art**, necromancy. See *Century Dictionary.*

21 : 23. **Misanthropy**, misanthropist.

22 : 11. **Laconically**, ironically.

22 : 16. **Progeny**, prodigy.

22 : 25. **Ingenuity**, ingenuousness.

22 : 26. **Supercilious**, superficial.

23 : 3. **Contagious**, contiguous.

23 : 4. **Orthodoxy**, orthography.

23 : 7. **Reprehend**, comprehend.

23 : 9. **Superstitious**, superfluous.

24 : 16. **Illegible**, ineligible.

25 : 1. **Intuition**, tuition, *i.e.* keeping or instruction.

25 : 21. **Malevolence**, benevolence.

25 : 23. **Locality**, loquacity.

26 : 16. **Paduasoy.**   A silk stuff named from Padua and the French word *soie*, meaning silk.

28 : 18. **Chairmen**, bearers of the sedan chairs. **Minority waiters**, " waiters out of employment, in humorous allusion to a political minority, as being out of office."

— Century Dictionary.

30 : 22. **Reversion**, " a right or hope of future possession or enjoyment."

34 : 6. **Mall.** The broad promenade, usually refers to the Mall in St. James Park, London.

34 : 24. **German Spa.** Originally a watering-place in Belgium, then any watering-place.

37 : 18. **Catches.** " An unaccompanied round for three or more voices, written as a continuous melody." **Glees.** " A composition for three or more solo voices, without accompaniment." — *Century Dictionary.*

39 : 25. **Looby,** obsolete for *lubber.*

40 : 20. **Frogs,** ornamented embroidered loops to secure the coat or cloak. **Tambours,** " a circular frame on which silk or other stuff is stretched for the purpose of being embroidered, so-called from the resemblance to a drum."

— *Century Dictionary.*

46 : 19. **Cox's Museum.** Popular exhibition of curiosities of the day. See Frances Burney's novel, *Evelina,* letter 23.

48 : 22. **Turnspit.** " A kind of dog of small size, formerly used to work a kind of treadmill-wheel, by means of which a spit was turned." — *Century Dictionary.*

50–15 : South Parade. At Bath. The Parade Coffee-house mentioned a few lines farther on was the North Parade.

66 : 18-19. **Accommodation,** recommendation. **Ingenuity,** ingenuousness.

67 : 10. **Ineffectual,** intellectual.

67 : 23. **Pine-apple of politeness,** pink of perfection.

68 : 7-17. **Exploded,** exposed (?). **Conjunctions,** injunctions. **Preposition,** proposition. **Particle,** article. **Hydrostatics,** hysterics. **Persisted,** desisted. **Interceded,** intercepted.

70 : 4–6. **Reprehend,** apprehend (?). **Oracular,** vernacular. **Derangement,** arrangement. **Epitaphs,** epithets.

76 : 10. **Allegory,** alligator.

78 : 2. Monkerony, a mistake by David for *macaroni*, a common word of that time for dandy.

78 : 3. Print-shops. Shops in which prints are sold.

78 : 20-1. Balancing, chasing, boring, terms used in dancing.

79 : 4. Coupee, a forward motion in dancing.

79. : 12. Allemandes, a lively dance, supposed to come from Germany.

79 : 18. Antegallican, opposed to what is Gallic or French.

80 : 7. Jack-a-lantern, will-o'-the-wisp.

83 : 2. I could do such deeds. Evidently a misquoting of Shakespeare's lines : —

> "Now could I drink hot blood,
> And do such bitter business."
> — *Hamlet*, III., 2, l. 408.

84 : 6. King's-Mead-Fields, toward the southwest of the city of Bath, formerly a part of the ancient royal demesne.

86 : 11. Quarter-staff or **short-staff.** Quarter-staff, " a long and stout staff formerly used as a weapon of defence and offence; so-called because in holding it, one hand was placed in the middle and the other between the middle and the end."

86 : 13. Sharps and snaps. " Sharpers."

90 : 5. St. George and the dragon. The patron saint of England. " Many legends were connected with his name during the Middle Ages, the most notable of which is the legend of his conquest with the dragon (devil) and the delivery from it of the king's daughter, Sabra (Church)."

93 : 1. **Caparisons,** comparisons.
93 : 8. **Physiognomy,** phraseology.
93 : 11. **Hesperian curls.**

" Hyperion's curls, the front of Jove himself,
An eye, like Mars, to threaten or command,
A station like the herald Mercury
New-lighted on a heaven-kissing hill."
— *Hamlet,* III., 4, l. 56 ff.

93 : 15. **Similitude,** simile.
95 : 9. **Affluence,** influence.
100 : 3. **Compilation,** appelation.
104 : 10. **Analyzed,** paralyzed.
108 : 14. **Spring Gardens,** favorite pleasure resort on the east side of the river.
120 : 9. **Ladder of ropes,** a ladder made of ropes, not an uncommon contrivance for the eloping lovers in romance.

" Know, noble lord, they have devis'd a mean
How he her chamber-window will ascend
And with a corded ladder fetch her down."
— *Two Gentlemen of Verona,* III., 1, l. 33 ff.

121 : 19–21. **Simulation,** dissimulation. **Antistrophe,** catastrophe.
122 : 18. **Perpendiculars,** particulars.
123 : 16. **Favour.** The early sense of the word, *look,* or *appearance.*
123 : 26. **Participate,** precipitate.
124 : 9. **Putrifactions,** petrifactions.
124 : 17. **Exhort,** escort. **Envoy,** convoy.

131 : 10. **Abbey,** the Abbey Church at Bath.

136 : 6. **Abbey,** as above.

139 :·19–21. **Dissolve,** solve. **Illuminate,** elucidate.

140 : 5. **Vandyke,** vandal.

142 : 7. **New Rooms,** " built in the Upper Four near
the circus, and there were complaints that the residents in
that position of the city were inclined to separate themselves
from their neighbors." — Aitken's note in Temple Classic
edition of *The Rivals.*

SCHOOL FOR SCANDAL

149 : Prologue. **Mrs. Crewe,** daughter of Fulke Greville
and wife of John Crewe, was a famous woman of Sheridan's
time. Her beauty was the subject of much comment
and admiration. The Crewe family and the Sheridans
became intimate friends.

150 : 8. **Amoret,** Mrs. Crewe. In Spenser's *Faerie
Queene* (Book III), Amoret, the twin sister of Belphœbe,
is the impersonation of the grace and charm of female
beauty.

150 : 19. **Reynolds, Sir Joshua** (1723–1792). One of
the interesting men of the eighteenth century, famous
portrait painter, member of the celebrated *Literary Club,*
first president of the Royal Academy, and author of the
Discourses on Art.

150 : 22. **Granby.** Lady Mary Isabella Somerset, daughter
of the Duke of Beaufort, married Marquis of Granby,
who afterwards became Duke of Rutland.

150 : 23. **Devon**. Georgina, Duchess of Devonshire, wife of the fifth Duke of Devonshire. A rival in beauty to the Marchioness of Granby, named in preceding line.

153 : 1. **Greville**. Mrs. Greville, wife of Fulke Greville and mother of Mrs. Crewe. Sheridan dedicated his famous burlesque *The Critic* to Mrs. Greville.

153 : 4. **Millar**. Another spelling for *Miller*. Lady Miller, the hostess of various literary assemblies at Bath in the eighteenth century. See Nettleton's Introduction to *The Major Dramas of Sheridan*, lxi–lxii.

154 : note. **Mr. Garrick**. David Garrick (1717–1779), the celebrated English actor, intimate friend of the great Englishmen of the time, manager for a time of the Drury Lane Theatre, famous for his presentation of *Richard III*.

154 : 5. Vapours, a term much used in the eighteenth century for " the blues."

154 : 8. **Quantum sufficit**. *As much as is sufficient*, sometimes abbreviated *q. s.* or *quant. suff.*

154 : 18. **Poz.** Slang abbreviation for *positive*. " Fine satire, that's certain."

155 : 3. **Grosvenor Square**, a fashionable square of London, east of Hyde Park, the residence of many famous people.

155 : 17. **Don Quixote**. Sheridan is here compared to the hero of the famous story written by Cervantes. There Don Quixote starts out to kill the " hydra " of the extravagant romance of chivalry; here Sheridan seeks the " hydra," Scandal.

156 : 1. **Mr. Snake**. The names of the characters and

the people mentioned in the play should be especially observed : Teazle, Surface, Crabtree, Backbite, Spunge, Snake, Careless, Mrs. Candour, Miss Verjuice, Widow Ochre, Mrs. Evergreen, Miss Simper, Mrs. Prim, Mrs. Pursy, Miss Sallow, Lady Stucco, Lady Sneerwell, Mrs. Ogle, Mr. Premium, Captain Boastall, Lady Brittle, Mrs. Clackitt, Mr. and Mrs. Honeymoon, Miss Tattle, Lord Buffalo, Sir Harry Bouquet, Tom Saunter, Lord Spindle, Thomas Splint, Mr. Nicket, Mrs. Drowzie, Miss Nicely, Lady Betty Curricle.

157 : 2. **Town and Country Magazine** appeared first in January, 1769. "The *tête-à-têtes* were a series of monthly sketches of fashionable intrigues published uninterruptedly from the first number down to the year of *The School for Scandal,* as well as thereafter." See Nettleton's edition, p. 289.

158 : 18. **Close with,** accede to, or agree to terms.

161 : 8. **Execution** corresponds to our sheriff's sale.

161 : 18. **Lud,** an oath, abbreviation for *Lord.*

161 : 20. **Egad,** a form of oath, using the name *God.*

166 : 11. **York mail,** the coach that carried the mail to York.

168 : 13. **Rebus.** An enigmatical representation of words by means of figures or pictures suggestive of them.

168 : 19. **Conversazione.** Italian for a meeting for conversation, especially on art or literary subjects.

169 : 15. **Petrarch's Laura.** A French lady celebrated in almost three hundred sonnets by the famous Italian poet, Petrarch (1304–1374).

169 : 16. **Waller's Sacharissa**. Lady Dorothy Sydney, celebrated by Edmund Waller, an English poet of the seventeenth century.

171 : 24. **Old Jewry**. A London street near the Bank of London, a famous resort of the Jews.

172 : 1. **Irish Tontine**. A system of life insurance named after its inventor, Lorenzo Tonti, an Italian banker of the seventeenth century. Owing to the defeat in 1773 of the Absentee Bill in the Irish House of Commons, a large sum amounting to £250,000 was raised by the method of Tontine Annuities and Stamp Duties. (Lecky's *History of England in the Eighteenth Century*, IV, 414.)

172 : 26. **Penchant**. From French *pencher*, to lean, incline; hence, a strong inclination, or decided liking.

180 : 8. **Pantheon**, originally the large building at Rome consecrated to the divine ancestors of the Julian family, later the church in Paris used as a mausoleum for illustrious Frenchmen. In this place, a large hall in Oxford Street, London, where were held concerts and various entertainments.

180 : 9. **Fête Champêtre**, an open air festival.

180 : 15. **Oons**, contraction for *God's wounds*.

181 : 12. **Pope Joan**. An old game of cards.

181 : 18. **Vis-à-vis**. French expression for *face to face*.

181 : 19. **Chair**. A sedan chair.

181 : 20. **Kensington Garden**. One of the public parks of London, extending on the west side of Hyde Park.

183 : 18. **Rid on a hurdle**. The cart upon which criminals were taken to execution.

316   *NOTES*

183 : 20. Clippers of reputation. " The figure of speech derived from the practice of clipping the edges of coins, a practice that led to milling the edges to prevent loss." See Nettleton's edition, p. 291.

185 : 8. Hyde Park, a very large park in London, the principal recreation ground of the city.

185 : 9. Duodecimo, here equivalent to *diminutive*.

185: 14. Macaronies. The popular name for dandies.

185 : 19. Phœbus. Epithet of Apollo; in ancient mythology the god of grace and beauty.

186 : 4. Piquet, a game of cards played between two persons with thirty-two cards.

188 : 13. Poor's-box. The box for receiving contributions for the poor.

189 : 20. Round the ring, a circle for riding, laid out in Hyde Park by Charles II. It became the fashionable riding place of London.

191 : 20. Spa, a watering place in Belgium, then applied to other places where there were mineral springs.

193 : 15. Law merchant, " mercantile law."

193 : 18. Indorsers, reference to the fact that the indorser of a note is responsible, if the original drawer fails to pay.

196 : 22. Ciscisbeo, Italian word meaning the gallant of a married woman.

199 : 6. Compound, compromise or make an adjustment.

201 : 24. Allons, French for *let us go*, or *come on.*

204 : 11. A heart to pity, etc., 2 *Henry IV.*, Act IV., sc. 4, 31–32.

"He hath a tear for pity, and a hand
Open as day for melting charity."

206 : 12. Crutched Friars. "A London street, not far from the Tower of London, named from an old Convent of Crossed or Crutched Friars (Fratres Sanctæ Crucis)."

— *Nettleton.*

209 : 1. Annuity Bill. In May, 1777, a bill was passed providing that all contracts with minors for annuities shall be void, and those procuring them, and solicitors charging more than ten shillings per cent, shall be subject to fine and imprisonment.

219 : 15. Post-obit, *post-obitus,* after death, "a bond given for the purpose of securing to the lender a sum of money on the death of some specified individual from whom the borrower has expectations." — *Century Dictionary.*

230 : 4. Race cups and corporation-bowls. "Gold or silver cups won at races ; bowls received as presents from the city."

232 : 6. Volontière grace. A French phrase for voluntarily or willingly.

234 : 16. Ex post facto. Latin expression for, *after the deed is done, retrospective.*

234 : 26. Duke of Marlborough (1650–1722). The famous general and statesman, commanding the British forces in the battles of the War of Spanish Succession. For him the palace of Blenheim was built near Oxford.

235 : 1. Malplaquet. A town in France where was won on September 11, 1708, the famous victory by the English, Dutch, and Austrian forces over the French.

318   *NOTES*

235 : 17. Kneller (1646–1723), a German English portrait painter. He served in England under the patronage of Charles II., James II., William, and Anne.

236 : 15. Woolsack, especially the cushion stuffed with wool on which the Lord Chancellor sits in the House of Lords.

270 : 20. Rupees . . . Pagodas. Coins of India. The rupee is a silver coin with a value of about fifty cents ; the pagoda is a gold coin of the value of about two dollars.

270 : 23. Avadavat. The strawberry finch, a small Indian song-bird.

277 : 18. Hartshorn. See note p. 12 on *sal volatile.*

278 : 1. Thrust in Segoon. Segoon is from the Latin *seconda.* In fencing, a parry thrust on the fencing floor. " Probably it was the *second* defensive position assumed by a swordsman after drawing his weapon."
— *Century Dictionary.*

278 : 20-21. Salthill. " It was formerly the custom for Eton school-boys to go every third year on Whit-Tuesday to Salt-Hill, a hillock on the Bath road, and there exact contributions, called *salt-money,* from spectators or passers-by to defray the university expenses of the senior scholars or school captain. (L. *processus ad montem,* going to the hill.) " See Nettleton's edition, p. 296.

291 : 16. A. B. at the Coffee-house. " A reference to appointments made at the coffee-house with intentional concealment of name." See Nettleton's edition, p. 296.

297 : 10. Licentiate. " The condition of having a license. Specifically in Central Europe, an academical dignity which in.tervenes between the baccalaureate and the doctorate, and is a step toward the doctor's degree."

— *Century Dictionary.*

301 : Epilogue. **Mr. Colman.** George Colman, manager of the Haymarket Theatre, and author of a number of plays.

301 : 5. **Bayes.** A dramatic coxcomb in the Duke of Buckingham's farce, *The Rehearsal* (1671). At first the ridicule was meant for Sir Robert Howard, afterwards for John Dryden, the famous English poet.

302 : 8. **Loo,** a game of cards. **Vole,** winning of all the tricks.

302 : 9. **Seven's the main.** A throw of the dice.

302 : 16. **Spadille.** French *spadille,* a small sword. In the game of ombre at cards, spadille was the ace of spades; pam, the knave of clubs; basto, the ace of clubs.

www.ingramcontent.com/pod-product-compliance
Lightning Source LLC
Chambersburg PA
CBHW031941080426
42735CB00007B/214